Retirement Planning

The Ultimate Guide to Being Prepared for Your Retirement

(Your Retirement Living Wealth Management and Saving Goals)

Clarence Young

Published By **John Kembrey**

Clarence Young

Retirement Planning: The Ultimate Guide to Being Prepared for Your Retirement (Your Retirement Living Wealth Management and Saving Goals)

ISBN   978-1-998901-65-4

No part of this guidbook shall be reproduced in any form without permission in writing from the publisher except in the case of brief quotations embodied in critical articles or reviews.

Legal & Disclaimer

Table of Contents

Chapter 1: Setting The Foundations For

Financial Independence

Congrats for starting this journey towards financial independence! When you're done with this book, you'll have the knowledge that you'll need to be able to declare that you're on the way to a more prosperous retirement.

So, before we go overboard we must lay the foundations to establish the framework by which we'll examine the idea that money is in the text, that is enriched by financial knowledge.

To manage the money so that it is working for you , not against you I will show you the fundamental concepts and ideas which are required to be successful. Financial literacy is an interesting matter since everybody intuitively assumes that they understand, but the data tell a different story.

It is believed that two-thirds of Americans are financially ineducated (Finra 2018.). It is important to begin learning about money at a young age or as soon as you can, since it can help you be more effective in managing your finances.

No matter what you do or where you travel, financial literacy is one of the most important things that can be applied to every aspect that you live. The main objective in financial knowledge is to help your money reach its maximum potential, so that your life doesn't get bogged down by breaks and bumps and gets speeded up to help you save time and enjoy your freedom from the money.

That's the premise behind the idea that money can be used to buy freedom. A lot of people are caught up by whatever is the perception they get about money and tend to view money in a negative way as oppressive and demanding.

But, even they cannot contest their bread and butter. To prevent this from happening an investigation into its primary characteristics and the impact it has on our lives must be done, which is the point where financial literacy comes into play.

To be able to spend more You must be able to exercise more control over your finances. Many people go through their lives, purchasing things that can be very costly to purchase like houses, cars and college education.

They're also packaged to us in order that we can pay for them in pieces over time, and sometimes years. What we don't know or at least not in the bold font is that the prices they are charging for are astronomical.

It's simple to allow things go this way, and then get involved in the one thing that's the most risky to building wealth: debt. When you have debt, it allows marketers to sell their products and services more quickly than they could without it.

What else do you think they'll be able to market cars with a high cost of $32,000? For student loans of more than $100,000? There is no reason to be surprised that debt is accepted by the society as a element of our lives even though it should be avoided with a vengeance.

In reality, it is now such a fundamental element life that the majority people do not see it as an issue, even though the debt of consumers reaches 15 million as of the moment of writing this. Many believe that debt is the key to the door to a better life but in reality, it's the only thing that keeps people from achieving financial freedom.

Before you make changes to your habits You must change your way of thinking in order to attain financial freedom. The first step in your financial education should be the realization that debt isn't normal. It should be viewed as nothing more than the infamous leeches that drain the potential of your capacity to accumulate wealth. This is why it is not a good idea to have it in your life.

However, life has its own vicissitudes, variations and fluctuations which means that there's no other option than to end up in debt. If you're already spending the majority of your income paying off debt, it is best to limit your spending to less than the amount you earn. This constitutes the second rule that we learn in our finance education. If you're looking to reduce your debt and increase your wealth then this is the method to follow.

If your lifestyle is out of your budget and you're living off borrowed funds or money that isn't yours and you are unable to sustain this lifestyle for a long period of time. Being over your budget will result in an arduous lifestyle and comes with many problems. When you make less money than what you earn, you not just reduce the amount of debt that you are currently carrying but also ensure that don't add additional debt. I'll go over these two concepts in depth and how to get rid of debt and also how to spend less than what you earn in the first strategy of chapter 3.

The money that you save through the process needs to be put to work - the fourth rule. This is the smartest and most sensible option you could make with your money. It will not only expand over time, but it'll also ensure your future today. To ensure that later in life, if you're in need of something, you won't have to go through debt to acquire it. I'll show you how to make smart investments with chapter 7.

These three concepts form the basis of financial literacy. They pop frequently because it is on them that the rest is constructed. If you stick to these three principles and organize your finances and life around them, financial security is not just guaranteed but it's a given.

The most important lessons to take away

This chapter is focused upon the significance of having a financial education in both your current and in the future. People who are able effectively manage money can go through the process of removing themselves from it in the fullest sense and be financially secure. The issue of consumer debt can be the root of all financial problems and should avoid at all cost. Spend more than what you make and stay within your means. And any savings you make should be put into a sound manner. With these points at hand, we can go ahead.

Chapter 2: The Easy 6 Step Process For
Effective Retirement Budgeting

T

The most obvious and disturbing reason for people not being in a position to effectively save for retirement is the fact that they do not budget for it. They leave it up to luck and take the approach of "going along with the flow. In the early of times, it is possible to do it without a problem. However, over time, the costs add up, and are classified incorrectly and mismanaged or ignored. This can be avoided by utilizing a basic knowledge of how to make a budget that is effective.

By having an annual budget that you want to control, it will be easy to keep track of your debts, expenses as well as savings and investments. Simply put, you'll be in charge of the flow of cash. If you're in control, no matter what the seas of the day are like You will be able to navigate through the waters and be in control of your financial situation.

Within this section, you'll learn how to build your retirement budget using six steps that are simple and efficient. So, let's get going.

Step 1: Calculate the amount you will need in retirement.

Let's first start by estimating how much you can anticipate having in your retirement. For this you need to add the amount you're expecting from these four sources:

* Retirement plans that are sponsored by employers

* Social security

* Personal savings

* Investments

Retirement plans sponsored by employers include the likes of 401kplans, 403b, and profit-share programs which you have heard of. If you're not aware that 401k retirement plans are provided by businesses to employees who contribute to their retirement plans by way of payroll deductions. Retirement plans 403b are offered by non-profit organizations for their employees.

However, profit-share plans permit employers to contribute to an employee's retirement account when they earn an income. However, this is at the decision that the company. If the business doesn't turn profits, the plan is not funded. the plan.

The Social Security program is an benefit program which uses the tax collected from the government of the United States to fund the trust fund for beneficiaries who are eligible. Who's eligible? Families of disabled those who have passed away and the ones who have retired form the people who are eligible for this program. If you're seeking an estimation of what you could expect out of this plan, a reliable online calculator can be found on the Social Security Administration website

(www.ssa.gov/benefits/calculators).

Finally, the amount that you have saved and invested which is what we're mostly worried about, will decide the extent to which you'll be able to live your retirement life to the fullest.

Step 2. Know your expenses

So, now that you have an what money you'll be able to retire with let's figure out what you'll require during your retirement. It will vary from person to individual. However there are some essential costs that your retirement account will be able to pay for. The sources of your income are likely to change after you retire, however many of these expenses will remain the same. The first step towards your ideal life is to identify your current expenses , not just your earnings. This is a fact that cannot be overemphasized If you aren't aware of the things you spend money to buy and how much your requirements are, you don't have a base from which to start.

The majority of people spend their time trying to save money without contemplating the amount of their monthly, annual or even their daily expenses are. As a result, they either don't save enough and end up suffering when they reach their senior years, or attempt to save more than they really need in a short amount of time and then blame themselves for not saving enough prior to. It is important to find the right middle ground between both so that you don't strain yourself too much while still accumulating a retirement fund that is beneficial to you.

If you're in the beginning stages of your career, or contemplating an adjustment to your career path in middle age, you're aware that the amount you earn will fluctuate. However, you are able to estimate the amount of your future expenses will be. To do this, you need to estimate the amount that you'll need throughout retirement.

I've made an Excel worksheet that you can use to determine the exact total amount in retirement savings you'll require based on your budget.

Let's take care of the most significant costs you're bound to encounter in your retirement. Costs for housing as well as transportation costs and food costs should be first priority on your list. There's a good chance that when you're retired , you won't have to take on any mortgages. But, that shouldn't be taken as a guarantee.

It is also possible to travel more often and utilize your retirement savings to fund and discover your hobbies that you could not do in your working life. It may not be an enormous amount, but it should have an appropriate space inside your financial plan for retiring.

This brings us to our necessity of food, and the costs associated with it. According to a 2017 survey of consumers, the cost for food costs increased by 2.5 per year. In spite of the slight increase this is one cost that undergoes small changes that are associated with the changing of diets and the aging process generally.

The second category should comprise the cost of insurance and taxes. Every tax-deductible source of income as well as your insurances on your home as well as health insurance, along with other important things to your household and you must be included under these categories.

Costs for personal items such as entertainment, utilities and clothing aren't to be overlooked also. The costs for healthcare, out-of-pocket medical expenses and prescriptions should be recorded since they form an expense category that will only increase as you the advancing years. Absolutely, aging is going be accompanied by difficulties. Even if you're healthy for the duration times of the time, your visits to the doctor or the hospital are likely to increase when compared to the current level.

Another aspect to determine is the amount of tax you will be required to pay on retirement earnings. In the beginning, you must determine an approximate tax rate. For instance, suppose you are in the tax bracket of 15% and the majority of your income is fully tax deductible.

This is the method by which you can determine the amount of taxes that you have to pay. The first step is to subtract 0.15 (the percent of taxes expressed in decimal) from 1. Then subtract it from your daily expenses. This will yield the amount of money you'll have to pay on costs for taxes as well as other expenditures.

If, for example, your annual expenses are $30,000

$30,000 / (1-0.15) = $35,294

This will provide you with the gross annual income that you need to cover your expenses and paying your taxes. In this instance you'll need approximately $36,000 of gross income to be able to retire comfortably. Divide this number by your tax rate , and you'll get an estimate of the amount you'll pay on taxes during retirement:

$35,294 $ 35,294 x 0.15 equals $5294 (estimated tax rate)

With these categories, you'll be able to cover a wide range of ground and relax knowing that your expenses have been documented and clearly identified.

Step 3. Apply the rule of 4%.

To determine how much savings you'll need to retire to be able to withdraw every year during your retirement, for not less than 30 years, without running out of cash and we've got the four percent rule.

All you need to do is to estimate your expenses for retirement, and then divide it by the 4%. This will give you an approximate estimation of the amount you will require in retirement.

However, the world isn't all good with this straightforward rule. One must be aware of the length of life one expects to live. If you're older it is important to make sure your portfolios are able to last longer and will be able to be able to cover the growing medical expense associated with it.

If the market is down, it is likely that the values of your investments will begin to plummet as well. Additionally, this rule is a requirement to stay loyal to it and continue to save until retirement. If you do not follow this rule during a specific year and make an expensive purchase then the consequences later on will be devastating.

If you believe you're not going to need the requirements of the aging process, then, of course you can clean your garage up and purchase an all-new Porsche. But , it's not recommended since it's likely to harm your primary sum, which could negatively impact the compound interest your retirement life is likely be based on.

Some think that the 4 percent rule as slightly more conservative. It is due to the fact that it was designed to account for the most extreme crisis or market declines like the one of 1929. If you're trying to remain afloat during the toughest times, this will be helpful even if the worth of your investments declines by a small amount.

But just because others are able to live lavishly , and with a higher expenditure percentage doesn't mean you shouldn't strive at it. Security and safety are two of the most important factors to take into consideration when you retire. If you find yourself in more tranquil financial times and a surplus of money, then that's only the cherry on top. This is one reason I suggest this old-fashioned retirement savings plan because it provides security in difficult times and can provide plenty of money should you be able to get through these funds.

4. Assume a two per cent inflation rate

Certain people who follow the principle of the four percent, keep their withdrawal rates at the same level. The annual rate of inflation as set for by the Federal Reserve is set at 2percent. The 4 percent rule allows retirees to be able to adjust to the annual rate of inflation of 2percent, it isn't much of a problem. However, you could also adjust to inflation and then withdraw your money based on actual inflation rates year after year.

If you want to adjust your withdrawals based on inflation rates that are actual will align your earnings to cost-of-living , my preferred method is to assume that the inflation rate is 2. The withdrawal rule of 4% with the assumed 2% inflation rate will provide you with an ongoing income. It's much easier to follow, is no less secure, and does not require a lot of calculations at the close of each year.

5. Allocate Money Using

the Bucket System

I have mentioned before how your financial savings will likely depend on your expenditures. Once we've got them down it is time to figure out what you can do to help save your earnings. The next question is, how can you direct the flow of cash from your income to be productive and increase your savings? To answer that question, you should be aware of the concept of an asset allocation framework'. What is that? Let's look at it in detail.

A asset is any thing worth its weight that is utilized to repay debts or commitments. The money you'd like in the near future must be invested in an asset that's assured of security that is cash. If you have funds that you don't require for more than 2 years, it is possible to put it in quality bonds. They offer a higher likelihood of a return than cash, particularly in the two-to-10 year period, with no many changes in value. Finally, any money you are sure you will not require can be put into stocks. They are not reliable for any time less than 10 years, however anything longer than 10 years and this is an asset class that is gold, so your gains will be multiplied. This method of distributing funds into assets according to the time frame is known as"the Bucket System, and is employed to control the retirement assets you have.

Here are five easy steps you must be aware of to create the asset-allocation plan:

#1: Know your portfolio spending needs

In the beginning, as I've mentioned before it is important to make an estimate of the amount you believe you'll require during your retirement years. People who save during their retirement years typically anticipate spending around 80 percent of their earnings during retirement. It could be less than the average for some of the biggest savers. If you're planning to lower your savings or reside in a lower-cost region of the nation the retirement costs will decrease substantially.

#2: Determine the viability of the estimated rate of spending

This is a crucial step since it can reveal how the spending amount you've come to is a good fit well for you, or is not. For this, you must divide your spending budget by your overall portfolio. If you are closer than 4 this is quite sensible. While you might be aware that the 4% rule may be a bit strict but as long as you're withdrawing less money in the down market and you can possibly withdraw more in times of prosperity then you're good.

#3 How much money should you keep (First Bucket)

Once we've assumed an essentially steady withdrawal rate, it is time to begin to assign our possessions to their appropriate spot. Any money needed in the coming years should be put in cash. This won't bring you any money however it will not change from its worth. Many of you want having two years of cash to spend However, you could make it as little to one month's worth.

#3a: Emergency Funds

A sudden expense is likely to occur. This could be car repairs or even a new roof or a costly trip to the vet like they do now while you're at work. There are two ways. One option is to plan ahead for your expenses during retirement. That additional amount will enable you to finance those costs. You can also create an emergency fund independent of your retirement account. If you opt for this option then you'll want you to add your emergency funds into the cash balance.

#4 What is the best amount to put into bond funds (Second Bucket)

It is not advisable for cash that is too large. The money you have can be better utilized. The money you'll need in the future that is more than three years old but less than ten years, should be put into bonds in order that they can earn some return. Normal inflation isn't a huge problem, particularly for a period of 2 years, so the purchasing power of your household will be retained. But, you should not put money into bonds for more than 10 years as inflation can be corrosive over the duration of 10 years or more.

#5 How much should you invest in stocks? (Third Bucket)

The remaining portion of your portfolio - and for that you have a time period of greater than 10 years, can be invested in high-quality assets. This includes stocks in the majority however, you could put your money into precious metals, property security and junk bonds. Be sure to invest in small amounts and diversify.

The three-bucket method has been proven repeatedly as an efficient and reliable method that has significantly increased your retirement accounts of many. This type of allocation can help your money serve you well and help you save for the future.

Step 6: Use a Retirement Calculator

Once you've got all the numbers and estimates I suggest that you get your retirement calculator out to determine a reasonable estimation of the amount you could expect to earn at the beginning of your retirement. But what do you need to be looking at?

The answer depends completely on you and a couple of aspects that exist in your daily life. One is your income at present and another is the type of lifestyle that you would like to live after retirement. Since we are known to become habitual, it is possible to confidently assume that a significant portion of your life after retirement will be similar to what you're currently living.

Once you've got all the vital data such as your income, estimated annual expenses, based on your life style The rule of 4%, and the inflation rate adjustment of 2% Enter the figures into the calculator online and discover the exact amount so that you can begin saving according to your needs.

The amount could be higher than you thought. However, there are many additional sources that can assist you with your retirement, specifically - an employer-sponsored retirement plan as well as social security. You can count on Social Security pension, Pension, or income from annuities to take care of some costs, or at the very least, the basic necessities of life , like utility bills, food and other small costs.

You can also get assistance from calculators online to calculate your retirement fund. One such calculator can be found on www.quicken.com/budget-calculator. This calculator will assist you in calculating the retirement costs based on your income and expenses in a simple way.

The most important lessons to take away

There are numerous deliverables we've covered throughout this section. In order to emphasize the key point, be aware of your costs first. This is the most important base for anyone since it reveals the amount you'll need to cover the essential things to you and important to your and your family's lives.

When you're considering your expenses should be a little higher, you must take into account the rate of inflation. This will give you an idea on the amount you should planning to save and invest in. The investment options include bonds and stocks however the need for an emergency savings account in place is essential. After you have a look at the numbers, you will have a good idea of the amount you can expect to spend on expenditures and savings.

Chapter 3: Top 2 Proven Tactics For
Successful Retirement Savings

R

Saving for retirement is a crucial prerequisite for living a healthy and fulfilling life in your older years. However, it's not talked about often, nor do most people really know about it. The result is that a lot of people live their life without even thinking about it or making enough effort to accumulate enough to fund their retirement.

Be assured that I'm here to fix this, and using just two simple and tried strategies, I will show you how to build the retirement funds you have saved.

Tactic 1: Change Spending Habits

If you're struggling to save money or always in the burden of debt, be aware that you're not the only one. Everyone around the world suffer from the same issues. Whatever they try, they not save enough. The thing that is odd is that the moment they receive a raise or get a huge amount or money they stay in the same position. If income isn't a major issue, then where do the issues lie? The majority of the time it's with how you spend.

Most people don't think that the very first thing to do in savings for the future is to change how the money they have is spent. It's not about the amount you earn, but rather how much and what you spend it. This is why you may always find you in debt, and struggling to reduce your expenses. If you're trying to alter your spending habits, I'll guide you on how to accomplish this and also how to establish sustainable spending habits.

You could think it's easier to say than done. That's true. However, it's not as difficult as you think that it would be.

The first step is to reconsider the way you spend your money and where it goes. To change your spending habits it is necessary to begin living below your budget. There is an inclination to spend to the amount of our earnings, and sometimes - - if you're really lucky - above it. When our income rises and we become more comfortable with spending more and even taking on more debt, or making lifestyle choices that are flashy.

To change this mentality, think about clearly describing what you wish to accomplish, i.e. saving enough money for retirement. It is essential to draw an idea of the things you would like and what you require.

Are things that you want for a while but you can live without such as ice cream. They are similar to the leafy green vegetables you are aware of as being good for the health of your body and mind. If you've covered your health with the greens, then you can enjoy as many ice creams and cakes you wish later on.

Naturally, your retirement savings and your green funds should serve as your main motivation and goal when you are in doubt that will remain in your side when you're going to do something reckless and destroy yourself by eating all the cake. Don't give up and give in to your desires, work for them.

If you live below your budget, you're guaranteed to have more saved to save for your retirement. This is among the most important areas that are will determine how you will do.

However the fact that you're spending less money doesn't need to mean you won't be able to live your life to the fullest or get what you want. Being in this manner will force you to prioritize and be deliberate with your expenditure. You must be careful when you spend money and purchase only things that are necessary in the short-term as you save to save for your retirement.

As you progress in your career and begin earning a decent income it's easy to become caught up trying to live lavishly. It is important to resist the temptations to go excessive while keeping the luxury in check. Instead, you should focus on saving the majority of your earnings. Don't give in to the pressure of a huge house or the cost of a car will make you more debt-ridden.

In order to live within your budget, make use of the monthly report you calculated earlier. Monitor your expenditure, and attempt to avoid unnecessary debt whenever you can.

Make sure you only purchase things that are important to you. Focus on you and stop trying to impress other people or competing with your friends. All these things are fine and good, however they will not do anything to save you money; in reality, they can only cause more financial hardship and debt.

If you are concerned about an expense that is major make a plan and save to cover the expense. The aim of saving at minimum 15% of your earnings is an ideal goal. Making less money every month and saving can help you pay off your debts more quickly and earlier.

To be paid back, debts could include car payment as well as credit card debts and mortgages. In all cases, it's recommended to pay off the creditors first. The reason for this is that interest rates on credit card debt can be extremely high, and this can be an enormous obstacle in reaching any other financial objective.

One of the best methods to repay debt is by using this Debt Avalanche method. This is the process of listing all your debts, including ones that have higher interest rates at the top and lower rates on the lowest. It is only necessary to pay the minimum on all your debts but only the one with high interest. You can then make use of the extra funds you have to make additional payments on the highest rate debt (Lorenzo 2020).

This way it is possible to quickly pay of those nagging high-interest debts before they get too far further down your list till the debts are cleared. This will allow you to speed up the repayment of your debt and get extra funds earlier to start saving to fund your retirement (Mcallister 2018.). The goal of settling the debt as quickly as you can ensure you do not end up burdened with debts during your retirement. This can cause it to be more difficult to enjoy your life to the fullest.

When you save less money and live in a budget it also means you have less obligations to pay in the future. It's just normal for people to feel better secured and financial stable when they're debt-free. Being financially free will result in less stress, greater self-confidence and a more enjoyable life in general. This is the result of your efforts which you must keep in mind to keep you on track.

The way your retirement plans pan in the end will determine to a significant extent by the way you manage your debts. Many retirees profit from clearing debt prior to retirement and may even view it as to be a financial goal of equal importance to the basic expenses of living.

My experience has shown that the main factors that can be a source of problems for retirees are the burden of debt, the lack of planning for the long term and a heavy reliance in Social Security. Any financial crisis can put their finances in chaos and cause them to fall further into the hole of uncertainty.

However, for certain people or even you, it might not be feasible to live a debt-free retirement. In this scenario, you must incorporate repayments into your retirement plan overall. It is essential to ensure that the payment of debts is an integral component of your budget, and not an extra, unrelated cost.

While doing this you should be mindful of the possibility of retiring earlier and exiting the game once you reach to the age of 50. The key is to be alert to new debt in this stage, as your repayment plans would require remaining active.

Do whatever steps you need to do in the months prior to retirement or after retirement to ensure that your debt is manageable and within limitations. For instance, you can contact the credit card company and negotiate the lowest interest rate or even a waiver of the charge.

Based on the kind of debt you've got it is possible for a refinance. However, prior to doing so you do that, it's important to identify the type of debt you're in. Certain debts are bad regardless of the reason including high-interest consumer debts such as car loans. They could hinder your efforts when you're not cautious about these. No matter what retirement plan you have it is recommended that these debts be the first things to get rid of.

However those with lower cost could be beneficial for you. When these debts pay off can improve your credit score or fico. Your credit score determines your risk for insurance and, in turn, your insurance cost.

In the same way, you could combine your debts by using a low-interest personal card. But, be aware of the risk of cost and hidden fees of debt consolidation deals.

If you settle your debts before they get to you it is possible to put off the cashing out of Social Security benefits until you reach 70 to get the best payout.

Social Security uses the money you pay in taxes to cover those who are beneficiaries under the plan. The money that is not used is transferred to the Social Security trust fund, which provides monthly payments to you during your retirement.

While you are able to start taking early retirement as young as threshold of 62 years old, benefits from this are diminished. When you reach your full retirement age, which is generally between 66 and 67, you will receive the full retirement benefits. If you're allowed to delay the benefits, those benefits will be increased by a specific percentage each month that you delay your benefits.

Tactic 2: Downsizing

In retirement, once your kids are grown-up and have an independent life What will you do with all the extra space in your home? Sure, there's an emotional connection to the house but is it worth the additional home insurance and property taxes that you will have to pay for the big home? It is possible to claim that the sentimental value and connection could be restored when you move to a different location with your family. However, the additional money that you have left will not be able to return. The decision to downsize becomes a pragmatic one to make in retirement.

It can be a great option if executed correctly. You will not only save more money but you'll also make life easier in various ways. Relocating to a more affordable house will lower utility bills and the home maintenance costs that come when you maintain an older home. The savings and the earnings earned can be invested into your retirement savings as well as a Roth IRA.

Naturally, downsizing is contingent on your personal specific circumstances. There are a variety of costs associated with it, and should be taken into consideration to determine if downsizing would be the best option for you.

The benefits of downsizing your home are certainly worth taking into consideration. The money you save will increase your retirement savings, aid to pay off debts fast, help reduce your expenses and also help you pay the mortgage off. The possibilities are endless?

The realities of aging should not be ignored when contemplating the possibility of downsizing. When people retire, they tend to live with less. However, sometimes, letting go of a house due to sentimental value makes the decision emotionally challenging.

However, downsizing may be a necessity because the retirement income might not be enough to cover the costs. However, downsizing needs to be done properly. First, you must is consider the costs associated with downsizing.

If you are selling your home it is important to receive the highest price for it. If you want to modernize your home it is possible take into consideration the costs related to repairs and refurbishment. In addition you may lose 6percent of the value due to commissions from realtors.

After you have sold, buying smaller homes and renting the property will have additional costs. Moving to your new house will also have its own expenses, like closing costs, moving expenses and other unforeseen expenses you might not have anticipated.

There are intangible expenses that aren't obvious but feel a lot. Your lifelong friends and the communities you were part of, and the doctors you established a connection with over time, these aren't simple to part with. It's difficult to make new relationships like you used to do, particularly as you enter your older years of life.

Selling your home can lead people to believe that it's worth more than what it is, in part because of the emotional investment that you've invested in the property. This is why it's crucial to have a real appraisal of the worth of the home prior to selling it. You should also think about having an appraisal from the real estate agent.

The choice to sell your home must take into consideration the above-mentioned costs associated with moving and see whether it makes sense. The cost comparison of the previous home to those of the current one are vital. Does the new home be more or less efficient in terms of utility expenses, for example? Does it mean longer trips to visit family members or get to work or to run around? Be aware of the cost of property taxes and insurance prior to making the move. Based on the location you decide to moveto, the cost differences could be huge.

If downsizing isn't an option you can afford and you'd like to keep living in the same house is fine. However, you should ensure your mortgage is paid off by at least five years prior to retiring. Making the mortgage payment prior to retirement is an enormous financial accomplishment, but it's not essential to eliminate all mortgage debt to enjoy a comfortable retirement.

In reality keeping up with the mortgage payment during your retirement makes sense when you have low interest rates on your mortgage. The lower interest rates are also altering the way that people view the mortgage payment in relation to their retirement plans. There are even benefits of the ability to keep your mortgage running during retirement.

A mortgage at retirement could help your portfolio expand as you earn more from the investments than your mortgage's interest. Of course, you must first evaluate the interest you pay for the mortgage with the expected returns on investments.

In this scenario it's best to lock in fixed rates instead of having an adjustable rate since rising rates could affect your retirement. The ability to continue paying your mortgage through retirement will lessen the burden of the other expenses.

If you are able to use the entirety of your money to settle your mortgage debt, you might not have enough money for unexpected expenses and might end up obtaining another loan to cover additional costs. Unexpected expenses related to health problems, can cause you to incur higher interest debts , which will reduce the benefits you typically reap by making your home mortgage payment.

You might also look at paying off other higher-interest debts prior to paying off your other higher-interest debts. Credit card and student loans obligations should be considered prioritised over mortgages, as the latter generally have lower interest rates when compared.

Taxes are an additional factor in deciding whether you should keep investing or pay off your mortgage. In light of the tax law, which was announced at the end of 2017, homeowners can't always reduce the amount of mortgage interest due to of the higher deductions. However, you may rather, get tax deductions when you invest your funds in retirement accounts.

Yes, the idea of paying off your mortgage before it's due is a great way to get satisfaction and an appearance of independence. However, sometimes you may be in the clear even if you do not pay off the mortgage, but save. The funds can be redirected to 401k, 403b and IRA to lower tax burden. The idea of putting money into an account in retirement or IRA is more advantageous than making a payment on a mortgage when needed.

It is important to remember that you're making the financial choice, and not just a personal one. While these decisions may be based on emotional reasons, must be evaluated as objectively. Certain people may want to feel peace of mind with no mortgage retirement.

I'm aware of many who do not like the idea of having to pay for an interest-bearing mortgage during their later years of retirement. The reasons may be many and each has their reasons, be it due to how they were taught or a natural aversion to risk, or simply following the principle that they don't want to have to pay back money, or having the satisfaction of not having debt.

It's not bad to pay your mortgage off prior to retirement, as I've mentioned previously. In fact, it's something desirable. However, if there are other issues that require greater attention than the mortgage payment then these other factors must take precedence.

You're sure you want to get your mortgage paid off as soon as you can even if the interest prices aren't as high and returns of your investment portfolios are stable. However, you need to be aware and be sure that you're making your decision by relying on your own emotions and are considering the math that underlie the whole concept and saving for the long run. Each person's situation is different and play a role in determining mortgage repayments.

Additional Tips

If you're in your retirement years, it's crucial to pay attention to your emergency savings in addition. At least the equivalent of 8 months' emergency funds and two years of fixed expenses since savings isn't only an ideal goal but also helps prepare you for market declines and other issues.

The money saved through downsizing could also be put in the high yield savings account. You can also invest your savings in a five-year certificate of deposit, also known as a CD to lock in the interest rate which usually does not change.

CDs and savings accounts help to protect your cash and pay you interest on top of that. They offer a variety of benefits which are essential to be aware of. Savings accounts allow you to withdraw money without penalty, and you can deposit the money at any time you'd like. But they shouldn't be considered a no-go for their use right now.

CDs are generally reliable interest rates, which usually don't fluctuate much in time. However when you are aware that rates are likely to rise, having an account for savings is more sensible. If the security of a stable interest rate is more appealing to you and you want to lock up your cash in CDs could be a great option.

But, you need to make a commitment to leave your money for a period of time within your account. The time periods can vary from one or two months (as as low as 3) to up to five years. If you sign up for longer durations the financial institution will offer a greater interest rate.

CDs are the best choice for you when you are aware that you are planning to purchase a major item. For instance, if realize that you'll need to pay for tuition in the next couple of years and you're looking for a long-term solution, a 20-month CD will help maximize your earnings from interest. If you have some spare money you don't plan to invest, a CD may be equally beneficial.

Interests are best when banks offer CDs. It's even more true when you choose to use longer-term CDs. When you consider all things considered, CD rates are higher than savings accounts. It is possible to determine how much you'll make in a particular time by using the fixed interest rates for CDs. Although you might not get the cash in the event that interest rates rise however, you might not be in danger if they fall.

Savings accounts on the other hand, permit the user to deposit and withdraw funds with no limitations. This makes them simple to work with and understand. If you're looking for cash as the only thing you require at any time the savings accounts are the best way to take. It is the perfect location to keep an emergency money reserve.

Savings accounts can start with small amounts and begin saving even with limited funds to begin with. In addition, you can decide to save a substantial amount of savings, if you'd like. However, CDs require at least a certain amount of money.

Rates on savings accounts are modified in times of economic climate has to be boosted. If rates increase they could allow you to receive more than what you are currently getting. If rates drop banks will react by offering lower rates. However the CD's earnings do not change.

It is possible to start by using both, and benefit from the benefits of savings accounts and CDs. It is also possible to test other options that can satisfy your requirements. It is advisable to have sufficient cash in your savings accounts to ensure you will have quick access to money when you need it without the risk of paying charges if you need to take them out immediately.

Important key

In the end, your budget will ultimately determine if you are able to save enough for the most rewarding times of your existence, or stutter in debt. The small changes you make today will accumulate and increase in time, getting the level you desire to be. A Debt Avalanche Method is the best method to reduce your debt and then eliminate it over an extremely short time.

The option of downsizing is one you could consider, which is both sensible and practical. It's not without its number of difficulties, however the end result is well worth it. There is no need to be forced to stay in a home in which your children lived, when you can simplify your life by relocating and selling or leasing it. Yes, sentiment has its place, but when all that is said and done you need to think about your choices and be able to do things that others don't.

The Debt Avalanche Method

Debt Balance Interest Rate

Debt 1 Highest interest rate

Debt 2 2nd most interest rate

3rd highest debt rate

Debt 4 Fourth highest interest rate

Debt 5 Fifth highest interest rate

Considerations for Downsizing

Pros Cons

Lower costs

(Low expenses for utilities and no mortgage payment) Connect with your emotions

(You are a fan of your home)

Cash from equity

(25 25 percent of your worth is located in your primary residence. It is possible to sell it and free it up.) It is impossible to get the same neighborhood.

Be Mortgage-free

(Do it only if can afford mortgages) Sentiment

(memories from the current residence)

More Options

(Trying out various locations and types of housing) Costs for transactions

(Selling home will result in expenses, such as fees, deposits and costs for moving.)

Easier to Maintain

(Maintenance expenses will be cut or (maintenance costs will be reduced or. The cleaning and maintenance will be lower in smaller homes.) Identity Change

Be more mindful of things

(Decluttering your current life and being more focused with your future purchasing) Less Storage

(Less room for things that you have currently or need in the near future)

Travel

(A smaller house will enable you to save money on travel, and you'll be less concerned about security) More difficult to host

(A smaller home will restrict the capacity to entertain guests)

Chapter 4: 3 Essential Things You Have To Know To Help Your Family Members In Need

T

The topic of finances and retirement could be an extremely personal issue. However, your financial freedom or independence will affect your entire family. Your parents, spouses or children, as well as grandparents will all influence your choices and this makes financial freedom during retirement a family concern not just a private one.

If you ensure that you're able to afford your expenses, you'll be able to take care of your needs without having to ask your children to carry the burden of caring for you. When you're financially self-sufficient you are able to aid family members who are in need. This is an important aspect that highlights how significant financial concerns for family members are.

Your Parents

Caregiving for parents can be a challenge especially if you're their sole inheritor. Even when you have siblings, you're probably aware that there's a sibling among you who is accountable for providing care and perhaps the sibling you have is yours. The study by Pew Research (2013) shows that 14% of adult at their mid-life have taken care of an elderly parent, and 70 percent of them claim they are either'very' or 'in a way' likely to care for their parents in the future.

If you're performing the bulk of the lifting, then you need to be on guard for certain things, other than burning out. Of course, any amount you put into caring for your parents will result in less savings to fund you own retirement. You'll end up in a perpetual cycle of dependence on retirement that can affect your children too as they'll be the ones who will take charge of you during your retirement.

It is possible to feel that you are being'sandwiched by demands coming from both sides , from your children and your parents in law and your elderly parents. The financial burden could be immense and you could suffer the loss of your income if only you are responsible for caring for your parents.

In addition, you're also likely to be facing increased cost of health insurance, particularly if are under 65. Your Medicare eligibility can only be extended until age 65, after which you will no longer be covered under the plan of your employer. What does this mean? The result will be higher costs and higher deductibles.

If you decide to leave your job to take care of your parents, you'll be further disadvantaged since your employer will no longer make any additional contribution to the 401K. Since your employer is only adding funds to the account of your 401K according to how much you put into it annually.

This means that the employer matches the contributions you make up to a specific limit is rendered invalid when you are forced to leave your job in order to help your parents. However, that's not all. Your other option, which is Social Security benefits, also is reduced when you're no longer earning work credit.

If you look at it from the various angles, making the decision to support your parents and take the care of them can seem like an unmanageable burden. There are many solutions available when you look for them and incorporate your children in the process.

The most effective way to avoid financial ruin is to ensure you're being compensated for your work as caregiver. If you've never experienced this before, you should talk to your siblings and parents (if there are any) regarding money.

It can be a cause of conflict in the family and is a difficult subject to discuss. However, it is important to discuss it regardless of how emotional the subject gets. You'll only create more problems for yourself in the event that you don't have a complete understanding of the financial situation of your siblings or parents who might need assist.

Find a suitable moment to ask your parents "what if" questions and scenarios that will stimulate them to talk and write the responses. Certain responses will be related to their health or living arrangements preferences, while some will be related to money. The more you learn about the way your family views financial matters and their desires include, the more you'll be to fulfill their wishes as best you can to your abilities.

A few of the questions you should ask your family is how mortgage or rent will be paid in the event that you decide to live the same household as your parents. Do not be shy about receiving reimbursement for any extra costs that could arise when you're looking after your parents. They could be the cost of food and medical care, transport and other living expenses.

You might also need to decide, as a family, if you'll be the primary caregiver with the help of other siblings, or are being expected to handle it all by yourself? What is the best way you and your family members going to split the burden? What is the best way for the money to be allocated and who will make the decisions? What percentage of your inheritance likely to change when you take on the majority of the caring? If you don't plan to leave your job, will the family let you hire aid? These are all questions that need to be discussed and addressed as a family.

It is possible to bring in an experienced elder law lawyer to create an agreement that clearly outlines the nature of your job and what your payments will be. Be sure to ensure that the contract contains all the information that you need to know, like your days off (when your children step in to help out with the caregiver's duties) as well as how you are paid for your work and the health insurance costs being due to the caretaker, and whether your family is required to help with them or assist with copayments and deductibles and copayments as well.

If you receive the salary you earn as a caretaker, the amount will depend on the resources the family is able to provide. However, regardless of what the sum could be, it ought be sufficient for you to make a minimum contribution of 6000 dollars (or $7000 if you're over 50) every year towards an Roth IRA.

If you're caretaker, you might be required to decrease the time you devote to your work in order to ensure that you provide the best care for your parents. You can, however, assist in your efforts to spend time with your beloved children and make sure they are taken care of appropriately.

You may be eligible for financial aid if you parent(s) have the capacity to qualify to be eligible for Medicaid. It is possible to avail Medicaid Cash and Counseling Programs that can provide you with direct payments that can be used to help pay for your time in caring of your parent. At present, this option is available in just 15 states, and you could be eligible to receive payment if the programs are in place for your particular state.

Home and community-based services programs, available on www.medicaid.gov/medicaid/home-community-based-services/index.html, also allow those Medicaid beneficiaries that receive in-home care to focus on providing quality care rather than worrying about financial problems.

If the person you love has an insurance policy for long-term care which covers caregivers, then you may be paid for your caring efforts. As per the American Association for Long-Term Care Insurance (AALTCI 2013) If your parents are covered by an insurance policy and its benefits include a caregiver's payment the burden can be reduced to an degree.

Check if your employer offers paid time off for caregivers. A growing number of families require at least one person to act as a caregiver for parents with a declining health condition and that is the reason why many companies are beginning to help their employees in this effort. If you take on the role as a caretaker when you work you could be eligible for an eldercare benefit.

The parents may also move to a smaller house and also benefit the entire family by selling the home. The money earned through this could be used to pay for the care payments. However, this also must be discussed. However If your parents want to stay at their current residence and want to stay there, they could consider the possibility of reverse mortgages.

Reverse mortgages transform a small portion of your equity in your home to cash. In this case, you're being paid by lenders, and the loan doesn't get paid unless you sell your home and move out or die. Be aware that this option is not recommended but is available to serve a purpose. It is tax-free, and doesn't impact the amount of your Medicare and Social Security payments. However, you need to maintain the home in good order when you are using reverse mortgage. If it's not maintained as it should be, and many have experienced it, then the loanee will foreclose on the reverse loan.

Children

Children, despite being our most important responsibility, they need to be taught how to maintain a an acceptable connection to money. It is crucial that they learn to discern between what they desire and what they require more often than not, satisfying the desires of their hearts deprives their children of the opportunity to discern the difference.

As you do have to, your children must be financially independent on their own. If they're grown and reside in your home, all you could do is solicit them to help out and share in household costs. This is an experience in learning throughout life.

In moments of stress you can help those in navigating through an emergencysituation, like the loss of a job, medical bill or a divorce that is costly or divorce, etc. As you ensure that it doesn't impact your retirement savings plan and you are able to manage it.

However, you must not allow them to rely on your account balance or they'll never stand the chance to learn manage their money, be shrewd and financially secure. All of this could have an impact on your retirement since you'll be putting them under pressure by helping them out while they themselves aren't financially independent.

If you have a child who is adult it is not a good idea to give the money to them. Money is certainly an ideal symbol for the love and affection of a child, however, it could also cause disruption. It is important to provide the children with enough funds to help them through a difficult situation, but not to the extent that it stifles their desire to be successful and to do their best.

Additionally, the money you invest in your adult child each year can help pay down your mortgage or credit card loans. It could also delay the getting your social security benefits until when you're 70, so that you have the most lucrative payout for you.

In the average American adults give their children approximately $7000 per year (Eisenberg (2018)). This amount, if correctly invested, could increase and earn dividends that can be used to cover various retirement expenses.

Adult children are able to remain in their parents' insurance plans until the age 26. However, they must be able to pay for a portion of their family's insurance costs, particularly those who are employed, as 82 percent (Miner 2020) (Miner, 2020) of the health coverage is provided by their employer as one coverage. If they aren't eligible to be covered under this policy in the job they hold, they could apply for coverage under the Affordable Care Act on .

The older they get younger, the less expensive the costs will be. In addition, if they've been working for a while or have started to work, they could qualify for a subsidy that could save you a significant amount of dollars. This is particularly relevant for parents with no children. When you move from the family plan to a single in addition, you will also enjoy less annual deductibles.

Grandchildren

Avoiding debt at all costs since it affects your emotional and financial security, particularly in retirement. There are times when people ask you to co-sign a loan on their behalf but you should never agree particularly with regard to student loans, as they cannot be discharged in bankruptcy. This is due to the fact that it could make you a debt slave for a long period of time if your grandchild has trouble paying for it in the future.

Co-signing loans may affect your Social Security checks until the loan is fully paid off. They also can stress family relationships. If they aren't paid off by the time you die and your child is left with a loan that is in default.

However, you don't need to be the grumpy old grandparent who doesn't want to be involved with their children's lives especially in the area of education. If you're working at a job, you must first ensure that your retirement savings are managed and that your balance on credit cards is in order and you have enough emergency money. It is then that you should begin saving for your grandchildren's college.

You can put aside money to pay for college for your grandchild through a 529 college savings fund. If the funds aren't sufficient, you might prefer exploring the federal student loan options that are that your grandchild can avail before thinking about a private loan. These loans are generally superior on many aspects like rates of interest and repayment plans and repayment plans, in comparison to the latter.

If your grandchild isn't suitable for a loan, and the credit union or bank refuses to approve the request, you must abandon the issue. There could be a plausible reason for why the loan was refused.

Discussing finances and money is an intimate family event and discussions should be held if you wish to make the process easier. It can be a difficult topic to talk about, particularly when you are with your family members. But, when your parents' lives, your retirement as well as your grandchildren's and children's lives depend on a well-thought-out decision and a clear future plan, it is crucial to hold money discussion on a regular regularly.

People who do not include their families members in the mix and who don't discuss about the financial situation of the family will be angry, arrogant and find themselves reacting to situations that they could have been prepared for them at the outset.

The most important lessons to take away

Doing nothing in the dark can lead to nothing; planning to the future, and planning your family's future, with everyone's involvement and delegated responsibility will be the best way to progress. Families that eat together remain together. However, you could equally be saying the same about financial planning.

Families who have plans to protect their finances can stay free of debt, fret much less and live longer and remain connected. It can be uncomfortable to discuss money with your family members since individuals react different ways to financial matters. Therefore, begin with small conversations about money. Ask them the questions that are subjective and 'what-if and let them discuss their thoughts and help you on the right path to take when it comes to money.

Being financially secure is not just about keeping you from being in debt and content and content, but it will also enable you to assist your children, parents, and grandkids in their daily lives. It might seem like a trivial thing, but it can be a huge help to your personal improvement in your daily life and also bring you inner peace.

Questions you can you ask family members, friends and yourself:

1. If I live along with Mom and Dad How will the mortgage be payed?

2. Does everyone feel safe Is everyone okay Mom and Dad are willing to reimburse me in some manner for the additional costs that will be incurred while taking care of their needs? These include medical bills, food as well as living expenses and transportation.

3. Are others able to assist when I am the main caretaker or am I required to handle everything? What is the best way for the responsibilities to be distributed? If I'm paid, will other employees get paid for the tasks they perform?

4. What decisions will be made about Mom and Dad's treatment? What will their funds be used? Who will be in charge of the finances?

5. How can I ensure that I am able to gain my own assistance? Do other family members assist me with breaks? What are my hobbies that keep me occupied when I am not working as caregiver? What can I do to earn money to spend time with my friends, or buy things I'd like?

6. Are you all okay with paying Mom or Dad's funds in order to provide for myself, even as being sole caregiver? If I perform everything, do I receive a different share from the estate? Does everyone agree to hiring assistance to care for Mom and Dad in the event that I don't leave my job?

7. If Dad and Mom would like to move into a senior home or assisted living facility What is the best way for this option to be made and how do we fund it?

8. If Dad and Mom don't have enough money will others be able to with their costs?

Chapter 5: Important Things To Be Aware Of To Avoid The Risk Of Losing Cash In Retirement

S

We now know the importance of financial security, the amount you need to save, and why this is a family issue. However, things can change with the flip of a pen and rates rise. Even if the economy does not have a major decline, interest rates tend to rise with time, and your savings are likely to lose value since the value of money decreases. What you can get for a single dollar thirty years ago could be worth a few 10-cent notes in the present.

You must put your money in a place where you are confident that its value will not decline and the sum is not subject to tax and penalty when you make withdrawals. In this section we will go over the basics of different types of accounts, the knowledge of which will preserve you in the security of your funds and aid you in achieving your goal of becoming financially secure.

Issues With Traditional Retirement Savings

The majority of people consider 401(k)s, 403(b)s, traditional IRAs and tax-deferred annuities as their most popular savings options for retirement. However these accounts have their own issues that no one is willing to discuss.

It's only in the latter years, when they must pay tax on these that they begin to realize the hassle they are in reality particularly when you are aware that your money for spending will be reduced due to the retirement savings being tax-exempt. There may be even taxes imposed that add to the burden.

The tax you pay during your retirement will result in smaller and smaller amounts that you are able to spend. This could rob you of the financial freedom you're hoping to attain during your retirement years.

The primary issue of traditional retirement accounts is that each dollar you save is tax-deductible. Butthat's not the only issue. If you own traditional retirement savings accounts It is also mandatory to take an account withdrawal under the requirements of Required Minimum

Distributions (RMD). The RMD is determined by taking the value of the traditional IRA and then dividing by the life expectancy. You can calculate what your RMD is by visiting schwab.com/ira/understand-iras/ira-calculators/rmd

If you were born prior to 30th June 1949 then you must take a minimum withdrawal before April 1st of the year after you reach 70 1/2 . If you're born after the 30th of June, 1949, you are required to withdraw a minimum amount before April 1st of the year turning 72. The more money you put into your savings account for retirement, the higher your tax bracket at the time you reach 70 1/2 and the higher you'll be required to pay taxes. This is the final thing you need to be trying to avoid and the declining value of your savings.

It is a requirement regardless of whether you wish to withdraw the money or not and it is regarded as normal income and taxed the same manner. If you do not make the minimum withdrawal that you are required to withdraw, you'll have to pay an amount equal to 50 percent of the amount of your RMD.

If you have plenty of savings within your conventional IRA the tax-deductible income will increase as it will raise your Medicare premium too. However, you'll be able to get rid of all the taxes when you retire when you place your money into an investment account that is tax-free like an Roth IRA since it is classed as an after-tax deduction and the payout in retirement is completely free.

Roth IRA

It's better to invest your savings into an account that offers more than what you put into or at least later on the road you'll need it. The Roth IRA is one such special retirement account that allows you to accomplish this. In the case of a Roth IRA, you pay taxes on the funds you deposit into the account. All withdrawals later on are tax-free. This is advantageous since the tax burden in the near future, during your retirement years, are likely to be more than the taxes currently.

However, be aware about the possibility that earn too much it could mean you are not qualified for it. The maximum for singles in 2020 is $139,000, and in the case of married couples it's $206,000. Also, you have a limit on the amount the contributions you are allowed to make to the Roth IRA every year. In 2020, the limit is $6000 for people who are less than fifty years of age. For those who are over 50 years old, it is $7000. old, it's $7000. The numbers change every year, so be sure to check the website to determine the highest amount you can save.

If you believe you're going to ascend in the tax structure for income A Roth IRA is especially advantageous. The amount of tax you pay in retirement will be more than the taxes you currently pay. If you begin early with your savings, the compound interest on your savings is likely to grow and you'll be able to maximize the tax savings. However, even if believe your tax rate is likely to be low in retirement, you'll continue to benefit from the benefits of your Roth IRA income , without needing to pay taxes.

Backdoor Roth IRA

There is an income threshold for an Roth IRA, you can think about the alternative Roth IRA if your income is excessive and you wish to avoid the income limits of the Roth IRA.

If that's the case, and you're earning an income that is substantial, establishing the alternative Roth IRA would be the best option for you. In order to do this, you'll must first deposit your funds into the traditional IRA and then convert it into an Roth IRA. It is possible to open an account for a Roth IRA account during the conversion process, if you don't have one.

Be aware that you'll be taxed upon conversion, as only post-tax dollars are eligible to be converted into Roth IRAs. After conversion, you'll need to wait five years (more about this in the following section) before you can take withdrawals tax-free even if older than 59 1/2 .

But, this isn't necessarily a wise choice particularly if you're looking to withdraw the funds within five months or less. If you don't put off five years before withdrawing the funds you'll be charged taxes as well as the penalty of 10. This is not a good idea when your withdrawals are likely put you into a tax bracket with higher income that the tax bracket you're in.

However, one thing you should keep in mind is that you shouldn't transfer funds out of your traditional 401k account that you haven't paid taxes to an Roth 401(k). If you're not sure if you should open the reverse-door Roth IRA or not, it is recommended to consult a certified Public Accountant who will give you the most appropriate advice suited to your specific financial situation.

Splitting the Budget

There are some advantages to tax-deferred investments and after-tax plans which include those offered by the Roth IRA. However, the latter appears to be a bit better than the former this is the reason a greater portion of your savings must be saved in this account.

Ideally, divide your retirement investment budget among tax-deferred retirement accounts, like 401(k) or 403(b) as well as an Roth IRA. Around fifteen percent of your retirement funds should be put in these plans. This can ensure that your savings grows and that your tax-free rebates will be in force during your retirement.

If your employer has an 401(k) match for employees, you should try to put as much money into it as you can in order to reap the full benefits of it. This, by itself, will give you the full 100 percent return on your investment and give your cash an extra boost. What's left over of the 15% should go to an Roth IRA. After retirement the entire amount becomes tax-free, which is exactly what you're supposed to be seeking out, so as to ensure that your funds are not getting into the wrong hands.

If your employer does not offer an 401(k) match I suggest that you first maximize each year's Roth IRA investment before you put money into the retirement plan offered by your employer.

It is also possible to leverage the advantages of a Roth IRA when your employer gives you an Roth 401(k) that matches any amount paid by you up until a specific amount. The match is to the same extent at the same time that conventional 401(k) programs are match. Both kinds that make up 401(k) programs are nearly identical in every aspect. There is only one difference when you have the case of a Roth 401(k) the contributions received to the plan are taxed at the time of making them instead of being taxed at the time of withdrawal.

The bottom line is that you do not need to contribute to traditional accounts in order to get the matched amount from your employer , if you're being offered the choice of an Roth IRA. You can simply make a contribution your money to your Roth IRA 401(k) provided by your employer, and you can enjoy tax-free withdrawals at retirement.

It's good to be aware that the traditional 401(k) plan can be converted into the Roth 401(k) scheme. However, once funds are in the Roth 401(k) program it is not possible to roll them back into the conventional 401(k) scheme. There are not all employers that offer the Roth 401(k) match because of the administrative hassle associated with the process. However, it's to be considered if your employer has one.

The greatest benefit of the benefits of a Roth IRA is that you can continue to maintain your account for a long time. There aren't any RMDs in this account and you are able to transfer the funds into your children's tax-free accounts when you die.

Traditional IRA Vs. Roth IRA - On Withdrawals

There are no RMDs in Roth IRAs as opposed to traditional IRAs. You are able to withdraw the Roth IRA contributions that you can make at any time, without paying any taxes or penalties and without giving any reason. But, this doesn't apply to withdrawals made on the earnings you earn.

You are able to withdraw your profits without penalty or taxed, if you're at 60 years of age, and you've had the account for not more than 5 years. This is known as the rule of five years. If you fail to meet one of these requirements or both, you'll be required to pay taxes or penalties on withdrawals.

In contrast in an traditional IRA it is 10% of the penalty as well as small taxes on any funds that you pull out of it.

Save on Taxable Pension

A pension that can help you enjoy your retirement is something that's appealing. However, retirees need to be tax-paying on their pensions also. However, where you reside decides whether you need to tax retirement income or not as the different states have different laws concerning pension income.

This is among the motives that lead people to consider moving their homes when they retire. If you've relocated your home of legal residency after retirement to a place that does not have a income tax on pensions or pensions, that state in which you received your pension benefits will not tax or chase you. If you were employed in California and now reside in Mississippi there is no reason to need to pay California any tax on your pension. This is an additional thing to consider to make sure that your retirement savings do not be wasted.

Key Takeaways

It is important to reiterate the benefits of the Roth IRA account. It offers huge tax benefits particularly if you feel your tax rate is likely to increase in the near future due to higher income. This includes tax-free growth of your funds that is compounded over time and tax-free withdrawals from your retirement times. In addition, you can take your retirement savings anytime, without giving any reason whatsoever, and all tax-free.

There is no minimum requirement for distributions also, which means that your funds safe. You can put money into the Roth IRA account using a low index mutual fund. It's a good option since index funds are inexpensive and come with minimal costs. The reason is that they aren't managed actively and you'll only be paying around 0.05 percent to 0.07 percent expense ratio or fees.

Traditional savings options, like those mentioned within this section, have served as the foundation to retirement planning for the majority of people in the last several years.

Butwith the changing times you must begin looking at alternative options, consider rethinking the ones that are already in place and make wise choices with a thorough review of all options.

Roth IRA triumphs over traditional ones, particularly in the event that you are aware that rates on interest are likely to rise in the coming years when you retire. Why not take advantage of the money you'd normally give away to pay taxes?

A great mix of most tried and tested options for saving and the more modern up-to-date options that allow you to profit from the tax differentials between the current tax rates and what they're likely to become in the near future is the best option.

There are differences in Traditional as well as Roth IRA

Traditional IRA Roth IRA

Contributions can be tax deductible

(Cannot contribute beyond an age limit of 70 1/2) Contributions aren't tax-deductible

(May help to extend an age limit of)

In general, they are tax deferred until the time they are withdrawn. Generally speaking the earnings are tax-deferred and tax-free upon withdrawal*

Income Requirements There is no income limit to contribute (deductibility may vary) A.G.I. must be less than certain thresholds.

Distributions Distributions are required by 70 1/2) There is no requirement to distribute at any time during your life

* Unless certain conditions are not fulfilled, in which penalty and taxes could be imposed.

Chapter 6: Ironclad Medical

Planning for Retirement

N

Nobody is eager to hear about their declining health and age but it's a fact that you have to accept and plan for. Even if all of your expenses remain similar, the expense of medical and healthcare bills will certainly increase.

This is the way things work. However, the situation isn't all doom and gloom . there are a variety of insurance plans that will pay for medical costs. Anything that isn't covered will have to be paid from your own pocket for which you must budget.

Make sure you are covered for your health insurance

Selecting an insurance policy to pay for medical expenses will differ based on what your medical needs are as well as what your financial situation. The cost of various insurance plans will also differ depending on the location you are looking. However, it's beneficial to have an notion of what the price will be to aid you in planning for it when you are making the retirement savings plan.

Two government-funded programs – Medicare and Medicaid which are intended to aid US citizens with covering their medical expenses. A bit of confusion could result from their similar sounding names. This is why I'm going to explain their distinctions as well as how they operate and the benefits they offer.

Medicare

It is an insurance plan that is available to citizens over 65 years old and for those with certain limitations. It covers hospitalization insurance and medical insurance, as well as additional insurance, and prescription drug coverage.

Of all these, hospitalization is among the most crucial elements since it applies to everyone over 65 years old, regardless of income. However it is important to note that the person who is insured (and your partner) must have paid tax on it for at least 10 years. Even if people don't pay a coinsurance, premiums and deductibles are still applicable.

If you're eligible then you're automatically covered by medical insurance. This applies to outpatient procedures and laboratory work appointments for a doctor visit, xrays, wheelchairs and surgeries, not to mention shots and disease screenings. In addition, you're qualified for dental, vision and hearing insurance.

Medicaid

It is a government program, which when in conjunction with states, assists people with low incomes of all ages in paying for health and other treatment. There are fifty different programs, with one for each state. You pay nothing for services included in the Medicaid program in your state.

However, there's an qualification issue that can render Medicaid unsuitable for those who are eligible. Only those who have more than just a few thousand dollars could be eligible for Medicaid. Medicaid program. There are some income limitations which differ from state states. The great thing about Medicaid is that the people who receive it stay in the program until they reach 65 and qualify to be eligible for Medicare.

While Medicaid benefits vary between states however, certain services are mandated from federal law. Federal government. This includes hospitalization, X-rays and appointments to the physician, nurse care, as well as laboratory and medical services. Additional services, including prescription medication coverage as well as physical therapy and dental care, could be offered from the local government. For the majority of Americans, Medicaid is used to pay for long-term health healthcare.

Buying Long-Term Care Insurance

However, you should not rely on government-sponsored insurance programs as they might not always cover long-term health care. In reality doctors are increasingly limiting the amount of Medicaid-insured patients each year. This makes accessing healthcare more difficult for those who are covered by Medicaid in comparison to those privately insured.

With the rising cost of the median medical cost the need for insurance for long-term health insurance makes more sense, as you would not want to cover all of it out of pockets since it will decrease the money you can save in retirement savings. With traditional long-term medical insurance, you'll be able to enjoy the benefits regardless of the kind of care you require and where you live. So, even in the final stages or end of life your long nursing home stay will not drain your savings or make you part of your estate.

When I look at the main reasons individuals purchase long-term medical insurance, two things spring to my mind: ensure that your savings are not eroding and offer you more choices regarding treatment. We have already stated you will stay secure and enable you to enjoy the best quality of healthcare , and will increase your life span and living quality. If you only have the government-sponsored insurances only, you can access the most limited number of nursing homes accepting the payments made by these programs.

However, insurance may not be accessible to all. I'd recommend that you not spend more than 5percent of your earnings for long-term medical insurance policies. In the end, while the cost of medical insurance is crucial however, it is not the only thing you need to consider in retirement that you shouldn't put off.

However, it is important to be aware that during your later days, Medicare won't cover all your medical expenses. Statistics show that the average couple who retired in 2018 will pay around $280,000 on health care for the rest years of their life. This is very significant for a lot of American citizens, and something you don't want to come from your pocket, or your retirement savings.

There are many healthcare expenses that are not covered by Medicare by itself. This is where the external insurance is required. It is best to obtain it earlier rather as opposed to later because when you reach a later age, insurance costs are likely to be high. The earlier you start as well as because your health will naturally be better in your younger years this means that the insurance premiums you will pay.

I believe this is the right option. It is because the cost of healthcare is predicted to rise in the coming years (CMS 2017). Every aspect of healthcare expenses, such as Medicare, Medicaid, private insurances, medical and surgical services, hospitals, as well as prescription medications are anticipated to increase. A portion of these are likely to be handled with the help of the federal government. However, the rest must be paid by the individual who requires the services when they retire and reach older age, that is you.

Health Savings Account (HSA)

A Health Savings Account can provide another option for healthcare coverage, and can be beneficial to you since it provides tax benefits. The amount of savings you can earn through this account makes it an ideal option for you. All in all, there are three tax benefits that you can enjoy including:

1. Pre-tax Contributions

In this system, each dollar you put into the HSA is tax-free. So, if you have any money put aside, you will have more money to spend on your medical costs.

2. Earnings tax-free

The money you earn in the account is tax-free. This allows you to get more money to cover medical expenses, if you require it. Even if your returns are small, the profits that are compounded over time will give you the funds to pay for medical expenses out of pocket. Additionally, since you aren't required to take money from your HSA until you actually require it, you are able to see your money grow in time, tax-free.

3. Tax-free withdrawals

Typically, when you contribute your funds to these accounts, such as an IRA or 401(k) then all money you withdraw is taxed. However, this is not the case when you use an HSA. When you take funds taken from an HSA account to pay for medical expenses the cash you withdraw isn't tax-deductible.

The savings that accumulate over time by these three HSA advantages will assist you in managing your current and, most important, your future healthcare expenses. If we assume your expenses will remain constant for the future 20 years, you can utilize your HSA to cover the entire medical expense you incur during your retirement.

If you want to calculate how much you can save up with HSA, you can use the HSA balance and tax savings calculator at bofa.wealthmsi.com/hsa/.

What that you put into your HSA can reduce the amount of your tax-deductible income. This means you can save cash that could have been used on taxes. It is possible to use the HSA to pay your medical expenses, but it's recommended to not touch it until when you retire. It will make sure that the savings is well-developed and, more, you'll be reimbursed for prior medical expense receipts you keep. This is a great bargain.

Let's look at the amount you can give to an HSA. There is a limit set by the IRS on the amount it is possible to contribute towards the HSA account, which includes the amount that is contributed by your employer, or anyone other person to the HSA each year. The maximum for 2020 amount you can give to an HSA is $350, and $7100 for your family. If you're over 55 you're eligible to put additional $1000 into the account of your HSA account.

It is important to know that there is an entry requirement to open the HSA account. According to federal guidelines, you may establish your own HSA account as well as contribute if:

#1: Choose a qualified high-deductible health insurance policy that meets the maximum out-of-pocket threshold as well as the minimum threshold for deductibles for the duration of the year.

#2 Don't take any other medical insurance.

#3: Don't have Medicare.

#4: You are not dependent on tax returns of anyone else.

#5: You are not eligible for any other healthcare savings plan, like the flexible spending account.

Health Savings Account (HSA) vs. Flexible Spending Account (FSA)

Each HSA as well as FSA are tax-deductible accounts that allow you to save money on medical expenses. A HSA account is only accessible to people who have an insurance plan with a high-deductible (or HDHP). HDHP). The minimum amount of deductible the healthcare plan has to be required to be considered an HDHP is set by the federal government, and includes the maximum amount one can make contributions to the HSA.

As stated above there is no need to pay taxes on money you take out of your HSA to pay for medical expenses. If you use the money for any other reason and you are subject to penalties tax. In addition, if you are already enrolled in Medicare then you will not be allowed make contributions to an HSA but you may use the funds to pay for other expenses, without having to pay taxes on it.

The Flexible Spending Account however is not available by yourself. It is only available as an option offered by your employer. The medical expenses that you're entitled to are the same as for the HSA. In this kind or savings plan, any funds you don't utilize at the close of the year is forfeited, except if your employer has chosen the possibility of rolling it over for you. However, even if they do the amount you are able to transfer to the following year's plan is restricted to $500 according to the IRS.

The money that is deposited into your FSA is derived from your pay check in regular amounts, minus taxation. However, the accounts are already funded prior to that. So, even if you're not paying in full, your amount you've selected at the time of enrollment will be available to use at the beginning each year. If you decide to quit work before year's over, you'll need pay back the money you've spent but which haven't been fully paid by deductions you receive from your earnings.

Picking one of the two options - that is the HSA as well as the FSA is a good decision for your finances. However, you can't have both. Both accounts could benefit you and can help you control your expenses out of pocket better throughout the duration of the year.

However, typically, people who are healthy and young with no medical issues or only have a handful of prescriptions usually do better when it comes to the HSA. This is because , although HDHPs are among the most affordable plans, there's an expensive out-of-pocket expense that can be as high as $16,000 per year for families.

This is a lot more than the amount you are able to put into your HSA. So, even if you are facing high medical expenses, you'll have to pay for a substantial sum out of your own pockets, even though you make the maximum contribution to your HSA.

There are a variety of alternative health care plans, which are more expensive each month, yet their initial cost is low. Therefore in the event of excessive medical expenses there are savings plans with a better plan than the HDHP which means you can get rid of the HSA.

However while the FSA isn't as flexible as the HSA The former can allow you to save cash, especially if it is combined with an employer-sponsored plan. The best way to go about it is to begin by determining how much you'd like to contribute. Determine how much you would like to pay for your deductibles, doctor's appointments and anticipated medical expenses.

In the end, the choice of taking or not having or both the HSA as well as the FSA is contingent upon the amount of healthcare costs you anticipate will be, the benefits your employer offers as well as whether or not you already have an insurance plan for healthcare that includes Medicare or Medicaid. The purpose of this is to make sure that your medical expenses are paid for and expense out of pocket is reduced even if they are not eliminated completely.

Whatever way you've been living your life over time things begin to deteriorate and become weak and eventually you're will require more assistance than in your younger years. However, if you continue paying costs of hospital visits as well as tests, medications and other basic healthcare services through your own pockets, you'll spend your savings quickly.

The most important lessons to take away

Health insurance shouldn't just be a possibility to look into at a later date. Take it up now while you're at the very least, healthier than you'll eventually be. This will lower your costs, allow greater access to services and make sure your savings won't be affected in any way.

Each of Medicaid and Medicare offer their own advantages. Both HSA or FSA are good alternatives to look into, principally due to tax rebates that you can get as well as the assurance that the money you invest is going return to you in the event that you require it.

Chapter 7: How To Build A Recession-Proof

Lifetime Source of Income

I

In the final years of retirement, one thing you don't want to see is a lapse in your earnings. However, the markets are not always performing well and cannot be relied upon for extended lengths of time. You need an income stream that is steady and is not dependent on the fluctuations and fluctuations from the marketplace.

Because costs of living will need to be paid and there's nothing more frustrating than seeing your life slowed because of financial issues even in the best of times. Therefore, you will need to put your money into investments and locate sources of income which are guaranteed to generate income regardless of what the market conditions are.

If you are able to work until you're 70 or can find sources of income to pay for your expenses, you could delay the date you start receiving Social Security benefits to ensure that you get the greatest benefits possible.

Part 1: Building your guaranteed

sources of income

Remember the costs we estimated at the end of Chapter 2? Whatever income sources you are able to draw from, you will be required to pay for these costs and make sure that it is covered to the fullest extent. These costs are essential to retirement, and are essential for your tranquility so that you can enjoy your work and your life to the fullest. If you're working today, you don't need to worry about tomorrow.

One of two sources you have as guaranteed income sources include those of your Social Security and Pension (if you have them). They are protected by your employer, the government or private insurance organizations and unions.

Sometimes, however, these options aren't enough to cover your essential and permanent costs of living. In these instances it's a good idea to look into an Annuity.

Annuities are one of the most effective alternatives that retirees can choose to use as income sources. If you asked an insurance company about annuities, you'll likely hear, "Annuities produce income that people can't outlive." It's bold, but is also the truth. Annuity payments can be for as long as you live or even longer , since they are based on your life expectation.

Annuities are one of the most frequently misunderstood financial products, and that's because there are numerous types of them. To say that you don't like annuities is similar to saying that you do not like eating out.

In essence In a nutshell, an annuity is not an investment, but rather an agreement with the insurer. The goal of the contract may depend on the type of expenses it covers, such as principal protection, long-term care plans for the future, or lifelong income. We'll focus on annuities for lifetime income since it is a guarantee of income in retirement.

If you've exhausted you IRA or 401(k) Annuities could assist you in finding more ways to save to fund your retirement. Because there are no limitations on contributions, you'll be able to save, save and save.

Another benefit is that annuities can be tax-deferred investments. When they reach their date of maturity, you aren't obliged to pay any taxes to the government until you cash out the amount that's. In this way, you'll have some control over the time you pay your taxes. If you put money into your annuity, you decrease the amount of Social Security taxes. With fewer withdrawals you will have less money which is tax-deductible.

Annuities may be flexible or fixed. We will however choose fixed annuities. This is due to the fact that with fixed annuities, you can know in advance the amount you are likely to earn once you start receiving annuity and the insurer begins to pay you. It is much better than putting money in corporate bonds or equity.

Annuity payments are paid out in lump sums with monthly either quarterly or annual payments. You may receive payments for a specified amount of time or for all time of your lives. The amount of money you receive will depend on the duration of the period of payment, in addition to other variables.

But, be cautious about buying poor annuity plans since many are offered by insurance companies just to collect a fee. It is not a good idea to sign up for the wrong deal if you could help to avoid it. That's why it's crucial to be aware of who you're getting the financial advice you need from. There are numerous insurance salesmen or financial advisers who try to trick individuals, particularly senior citizens at different stages of retirement, to buy annuities. It is important to tailor the advice for your personal financial situation and not based on the stock market plan only available for sale. (You will be taught how to select the best adviser in Chapter 9).

However, they aren't intended for all. The reason I mention this is because they have very high costs. The fees they charge are quite high in comparison to mutual funds and CDs. The cost of commissions and fees can make the form of a significant cost.

A fixed income annuity not a good option in the event that you don't really need the money at the moment. If you feel you're in greater need of cash now than later when you retire, then you ought to consider immediately an annuity.

An immediate annuity is when you can convert the lump sum of money to an income stream. If you decide to purchase an instant annuity, ensure that you get estimates of how much of the the payment is tax-free. If you wish to receive the money prior to retirement then a deferred annuity ought to be your first choice. The only distinction between a deferred and an immediate annuities is the time the time when the repayment phase of the annuity commences.

An annuity that is deferred has an accumulation time, but immediate annuities don'thave one, as the name implies. When deferred annuities need you to make a set of payments or put them off until the future, immediate annuities can be paid out in one lump amount.

You can contribute at any time for both Both will offer uninterrupted payments throughout your life.

However, I wouldn't suggest them if you're not planning to retire at the moment, as the interest rates will rise in the near future. This is because there isn't much to make much from these annuities, as the increase in interest rates could render them useless. If you're not in retirement today, immediate and deferred annuities do not make sense. For the vast majority of people and the majority of people, a fixed-income annuity is the best choice.

Whatever insurance company you purchase annuities from, you must make sure that they're in good financial standing. Don't forget to examine their financial ratings. The approval of rating firms is usually used to evaluate the financial condition and functioning of the business.

There's another kind of annuity to be aware of: the QLAC, which stands for Qualified Longevity Contract QLAC, also known as. It is a particular kind of annuity that is designed for people who don't suffer from any serious health issues and can be sure to live into their 90s and possibly even crossing the threshold of 100 years. The longevity-based annuity can be purchased using tax-deferred savings.

QLAC lets you commit to pay a portion of your money today in exchange for a monthly payment which begins at some point in the near future. What's the reason? It's because you want to lower the possibility of your expenses becoming without payment in retirement. You would like to have a guaranteed income that isn't cut short. It's similar to a pension you purchase for yourself.

Of all the annuities and other retirement options This is the only one which allows you to delay your income-related repayments until 85 years old. This means you can delay the minimum distributions for the IRAs and 401(k)s after 72 years of age.

The bottom line is that an annuity serves as an investment as well as is an insurance plan. You may be wary of purchasing an annuity as you're concerned about your death before receiving the amount equal to or more than your investment. But, with an annuity you get some kind of insurance policy, similar to health insurance. If you buy it, you will receive the income you will receive in retirement regardless of what happens.

Part 2: Financing your retirement

and an additional side hustle

An opportunity to earn extra money is not the first thing people consider when they think about ways to earn an assured source of income. However, the current economic climate has opened up opportunities as well as some unique and innovative ways to earn money that many have taken advantage of. Of of course, having a side hustle can be scary but it's definitely worthy of the time and effort.

The great thing about this is you do not need to take on anything new. You can use the skills you already possess. Although people love to think about things that are totally different when they retire Most people choose to do a side-job using their current skills and talents, which is a smart choice. You don't have to learn anything , and you can keep the money flowing.

It's not a bad thing, you don't need to follow exactly the same thing you did prior to. You can, however, draw on your experience in your work. If you're not sure which of your abilities you can use, create your list of tasks you are confident you can accomplish. Examine the items you've listed and ask yourself "Which of these interests me and which ones could I master to make it beneficial to other people? Choose from the items that are typical.

A majority of people have a side hustle. However, while the majority of people make it an extra job, there's no requirement to be employed full-time before you can start working in the background. With the gig economy, everything's an opportunity to make money on the side.

Because retirees typically have more time to pursue side ventures and side hustles, they are able to earn significantly more money, too. If you're not sure what to do then let's look at some suggestions you could try.

Care for pets

If you're a good pet owner and are a good pet lover, you could be a pet sitter because there's always a need for trustworthy people to look after their pets when they're absent. Based on the type of contract you have for your clients, you may walk their pets and feed them. You can also perform other tasks.

Clinical Trials

The medical research studies on the elderly population are constantly being funded by clinical research. You could earn some money by participating in research for which you're qualified. Certain trials could be as easy as observing and analyzing daily habits like diet or sleep. Some may request that you use medications that are connected to your health condition.

If you're near a research center or research center, then clinical trials may be a breeze to be a part of. Many of these opportunities are paid at or above minimum salary. Since the jobs tend to be routine it's a good opportunity to earn some money without having to return to working.

Renting Space

If you have plenty of room in your house like retirees have, you could quickly turn a portion of it into an excellent way to earn income. Of course, this is contingent on the dimensions of the room and its overall quality as well as the need in your area. It is possible to provide storage space only and earn money without having to do any activities other than at the beginning and the at the end of the contract. However, if the space is only used for storage, your earning are limited.

Substitute Teacher

Teaching isn't suitable for everyone, but working as substitutes will enable you to sharpen your skills and aid children in learning without the obligation of committing to a full schedule or other complex aspect of teaching. If you'd like to set your own hours, show students the things you already know and make a decent salary This is the ideal solution for you.

While there are no federal guidelines for substitute teachers be sure to verify the regulations your state has in place. Schools and districts could have specific rules and regulations that you must be aware of.

There are a few points to consider before you start your side hustle, and you should make sure that it runs smoothly and doesn't become a gruelling work.

1. Learn about the prerequisites for a small-sized business If you're planning to start an enterprise that is small you must obtain an enterprise license. To get this license, you'll be required to inquire with your department of commerce in your state. If your venture grows, you should create a limited liability corporation (or LLC) to protect your assets from lawsuits.

2. Be aware of your limits It isn't a good idea to be exposed to risks that you're not prepared for or which are beyond the limits of your control. If you enjoy children just for a brief period do not put yourself through long hours at school. If you prefer small pets, you should only be able to pet-sit those with smaller sizes.

3. Be cautious of the creepy gigs It is tempting to accept any job that is given to you, especially at the beginning. However, this will only multiply the work and make it seem like full-time jobs eventually making you exhausted.

4. Be on the same page If you're married or have an a spouse or partner ensure that they're in agreement in what you're doing and how much. You and your partner can explore side hustles you can work on together to take on the same burden and reduce the chance of burning out.

A lack of a reliable source of income could be quite a problem during retirement, particularly if your investments are tied to the fluctuation of the market. With an annuity that is fixed income and some side hustles, you'll be able to relax knowing that your expenses will be paid for and you won't fall into debt.

Important lessons to take away

Being able to count on a reliable source of income when you retire is possibly the most important option to ensure your future.

Annuities are ideal in that aspect because you can determine how your funds will be returned for you later in the near future. There are a variety of annuities however the fixed income one is the one I strongly recommend, since it is specifically designed for people who wish to generate income that is not influenced by disruptions to the market or disruptions within your own life.

Annuities that are deferred or immediate are considered due to their distinctive benefits. Apart from that there are many other ways to earn you a steady stream of income when you retire. It's true that you wouldn't wish to start the responsibility of a new job. So ensure that you are enjoying the work and don't do too much in case you don't find the right fit for you.

Comparison amongst Annuities

Fixed Annuity Indexed Annuity Variable Annuity

Rate of Return Lower tax-deferred growth Fixed interest rate that is set in advance. Higher possibility of growth than fixed annuities interest rates are not disclosed in advance. More chance for tax-deferred growth, with the potential for loss

Risk Factors Locked-in for a period of one plus years. Minimum guarantee accumulation age. Maximum Guaranteed Interest Rate Risks associated with each sub-account

Tax-Deferral Yes Yes Yes

Who Benefits Anyone looking to take on lower risk and those who seek to increase their upside potential while ensuring a guarantee of a guaranteed interest rate are willing to accept a higher amount of risk to higher upside potential

Chapter 8: The 4 Pillars Of Smart Investing

SMart people are aware of how and where to invest and when to invest and which options can be beneficial to them not only in the immediate future, but in the long run in life too. There's no reason to invest money if you'll need to come up with additional sources of income that are greater than the amount you've put in, particularly in the later years.

It is important to plan your investment with longevity with longevity in the back of your head. If you don't have any medical condition that ensures that you will live a shorter time and you must plan for investing with the assumption that you'll be alive at the very least until 100. In the present situation of healthcare and medical technology, living to 100 years old is feasible and extremely likely. Anyone who doesn't have any existing, possibly harmful condition could be confident about getting to the three-digit mark.

It was simple to make the smart choice in the past, however in this decade, you must begin investing wisely prior to the time when things change and new trends should be taken into consideration. When investing, be mindful of this Russian phrase in mind"Trust but verify".

Pillar No.1 : Know Your End Goal

The first step to investing wisely is to know what is important to you most. That is your ultimate goal. When you are focused on what is crucial in your life, which is savings for retirement in our instance and you manage your time, energy and money in a wise way and try to avoid getting sucked by the many distractions. It is essential to save enough'. There isn't a absolute rule that requires you to save this amount or more. The amount you can save will be determined by what your expectations for expenses will be. Based on your goals You will be able to determine what the average amount you'd prefer to have at retirement and that will affect the way you distribute your money.

The way you allocate your funds is the most crucial decision you'll have to make because it will determine the success on your portfolio. It's even more crucial than choosing the best security. The distribution of assets isn't fixed and can be adjusted in response results and failures along course. In the end, goals shift over time, and it can be difficult to navigate the financial landscape.

Pillar No.2 : Risk Level

There is some risk associated with each asset allocation decision you make. There is a risk inherent to the investment you make, as you anticipate to make returns that will help you reach your goals. The choice you take must be in line with your 'risk-preference' or risk capacity. When you make an investment decision make it based on the following three factors:

1. Is it within your ability to accept this risk?

#2: How do you take the best risk?

#3 What is the lowest price at which you could accept this risk?

There are times where you shouldn't be taking the risk necessary to accomplish your goals since you do not have the capacity to take it. There is a point in every person's existence when risk tolerance is very low, and the stakes are high. Don't gamble your entire savings savings at this point that is 5-10 years prior to retirement This period is worthy of the name "Risk Zone'.

There's a significant chance that, if you fail to make a profit in this time frame, you'll to lose a substantial amount that could impact your retirement plan. This could reduce the amount of time that your savings lasts, even if markets fail to rebound. The key to a smart allocation of assets is being able to accept the risks that are necessary, particularly in the risk Zone.

Pillar No.3 : Diversify!

The third pillar suggests that the best thing you can do when you're planning for investment is diversify the portfolio of your investments as wide as you can. This means investing in commodities, real estate as well as bonds and global stocks as well as other bonds. When you're in the Risk Zone, the best way to manage your risk is to manage your risk by using safe assets, such as Treasury Bills. This can be achieved by avoiding the addition of more bonds. In the end, you need to look for an array of risky and secure assets. The ability to manage risk and diversify your portfolio will give you the most lucrative returns on the risks you are willing to take over the course of time.

Pillar No.4 : Be Cost Conscious

The third pillar, which is being conscious of costs - is simple common sense. If you are spending more money the returns are likely to be less. Investors are now looking to diversify their portfolios and reduce costs. This has led them to invest in passive indexes, like the Exchange-Traded Funds (ETFs). It is also possible to consider it for improving your return.

A smart allocation of assets requires taking the risk one is an ability to handle, especially given the age of one's. The risk capacity should not be overlooked because it can lead to disastrous failures. In reality, the majority of retirement savings don't go to waste because of investment losses. They're at risk due to huge losses in investment when they're not the right time when they're in that Risk Zone, or the transition from working to retirement.

Assume an inflation of 3%. rate

The amount you're likely to receive is contingent upon the return rate on your investment. Just a tiny difference in the rate you're expecting to earn can affect how much you'll need to save to fund your retirement.

In the majority of cases the inflation rates within the U.S. have fluctuated between 1.5 to 4% annually. That means when you receive an average return of 10% for your investment during an year with 3percent inflation rate however, your actual returns are close to 7% adjusted to inflation. It's important to understand that inflation could be the main reason one isn't able to put money into your savings account and believe that it will grow forever. In the event that your earning is 2.2%, and inflation rate is 3percent, your money is declining in value in other words, you're losing money.

The length of time you put aside for investing will impact the amount of return you'll earn. If you have more time to invest it, you are able to be more proactive in the way you invest your money and choose stocks over other investment options that yield high returns.

If you make investments over the long haul and you're patient, you'll also enjoy better years that will hopefully make up for the negative ones. That's why it's important to not quit the market immediately upon the first sign of a slump, as you'll miss the opportunity to profit when markets rebound.

To stay ahead of the increasing inflation and rate, it's advisable to put money into stocks. Over the years, stocks have in general delivered investors with gains that are far above the rate of inflation.

As previously mentioned, US treasury bonds also tend to be more stable with inflation, particularly when contrasted with cash. However, they don't give a substantial increase in inflation like stocks do. But, they're more secure than stocks, and is always a safe option.

A balanced mix of stocks and bonds within your investment portfolio can give you a the feeling of emotional and financial security. Bonds can protect you on the market and you continue to invest your money into stocks and reap huge profits in the event of a bear market.

For a healthy return on your investments, you need to be able to implement a sound strategy for asset allocation. In the past, investors utilized the old heuristic of they had to subtract their age by 100. whatever result they get is the percentage of their portfolio should be invested in stocks. For example, if you're 30 you're investing 70 percent of your portfolio into stocks. However, if you're aged 70, you'll invest 30%.

However, the lives spans across the globe are increasing as people live longer. I suggest you alter the rule little and reduce your age between 110 and 120. The resulting amount should be the proportion of your portfolio where is invested in stocks. The reason behind this is that you want your investment to last for a longer time and to do this, you'll require the additional growth which only stocks can offer.

Over the years retired people were advised to mix 60 percent of their portfolios equity and the remaining 40% with bonds. They were considered to be well-balanced portfolios and performed well in the 1980s and 90s.

However traditionally low rates of interest and a series of bear markets after 2000 have reduced the worth of this 60/40 method. Today, a balanced portfolio should comprise more than just bonds and stocks.

A few of the latest alternatives you can be looking to include in your portfolio are commodities, private equity and hedge fund. Another addition that will boost your portfolio are inflation-proofed investments that you could consider. You should make sure the eggs you have are spread in different baskets.

It is not enough to make a bet on one future. While it was easy to adopt the 60/40 rule due to the simplicity and convenience it offered however, bonds and stocks alone are not able to provide you with the income you need and also protect you from the effects of inflation and market declines anymore.

Diversification

Diversification appears to be the rule in the business. If you're going through bonds and stocks be sure to have a diverse portfolio of them. If you are investing in stocks, make sure you invest in not just one , but about 25 stocks, and make sure that no stock is more than four percent of your total portfolio of stocks.

Anything over 4% will mean you're risking too much on just one investment. Also, as retirees you should not be trying to increase the risk of any investment. The amount you invest in stocks could be divided further into broad US Market ETF, dividend paying stocks and a broad international ETF. The percentages of each can be divided into:

"Broad global US market for ETFs - 65 %

* Dividend-paying stock - 20 percent

* International ETF with broad total * 15 percent

Mutual funds are an alternative investment option. However, they're only suitable when you're looking for an investment that isn't loaded. Are you thinking about what a no-load mutual fund can be? It is a kind of mutual fund where the shares can be sold with out a middleman generating commissions or sales charges. This is in stark contrast to a fund with a level load that requires the buyer to pay fees for the time they have the fund.

We're after all seeking investments that are less costly to reduce the amount you'll need to invest in order to reap massive return. Here's the place the expense ratio of Mutual Funds comes into play.

The expense ratio is the present cost of investing into an ETF or mutual fund. It's dependent on the amount of money you invest into the fund. For instance, if you invest with a fund that has an expense ratio of 1 percent, and you put in $1000, you must pay 10 dollars as a annual fee. This fee covers the operation of the fund, which is the amount you pay for other investors to select the best investment fund.

There's no way around it since every ETF and mutual fund comes with an expenses ratio. It's nevertheless important to ensure there's no overpayment than you need to. However, the issue is what's the best price to pay for this cost proportion?

Fortunately, expenses ratios are in declining and that's an excellent thing for all. However, finding the cost ratio of mutual funds is an extremely difficult task. This is especially true for 401(k)s because the cost is not upfront and you must look up this.

If you're working with the 401(k) check to the list of all the investment options included inside your 401(k) and the costs from the HR department. In most cases you'll see all the expense ratios for all the funds available within the 401(k).

However, if you're fortunate enough to be able to obtain it and end up with only junk funds You must investigate further. What do you need to do to discover the ticker symbol of each fund that is an alternative? It's an alphabet string like VFINX, for Vanguard's mutual fund's S&P 500.

When you've found that ticker symbol you will be able to discover the expense ratio for any fund. Similar to finding the ticker symbol of the fund to determine its expense ratio could be applied to the healthcare savings plan, IRA as well as other types of.

If you're not ready to let your income stream to fluctuate due to the fluctuation of the market, then it is time pay attention to the alternatives to invest that are more conservative and safeguard your investments that aren't as unpredictable. One option is the ETF.

It is understandable that retirees opt for these options because they do not have as long an horizon of time ahead of them as young people, who have the ability to take on greater risks. But it is important to diversify your portfolio to ensure that no market crash can affect your portfolio detrimentally. This is the reason why the range of securities, that is the ETFs which trade similar to stocks traded on exchanges could be an attractive alternative to think about.

With ETFs, you must have a buffer in place to cover inflation, travel medical expenses or even just as a protection. Therefore, if you're looking for about four percent of your income from your portfolio, you need to increase the amount to around 7 percent. The difference between your income and the actual income you earn should be sufficient to cover the buffer you're trying to keep.

It is important to know what you need like the basic necessities, medical costs and emergency funds that have inflation in mind because it directly relates to the risk you be required to take to achieve those returns. It even ties into and affects your allocation of assets as well as the type of ETF you will ultimately purchase.

After you have divided your assets to stocks, bonds, and other income-generating assets, and pushed them to their potential, you can begin searching to find an ETF that matches your income goals and is likely to achieve your goal of total return.

There are some things to be aware of when you put the money you have in an ETF. Although most ETFs are less expensive in terms of fees than mutual funds this isn't always the scenario. Certain ETFs, such as Teucrium Sugar ETF. Teucrium Sugar ETF, have an even higher fee with having an expense ratio of 2.92 percent, which is higher than that of the Vanguard Total Stock Market ETF which has a far more profitable 0.03 percentage expense ratio. Although a small proportion of ETFs charge charges that are higher than one percent, it is not wise to believe that ETFs are always less expensive than mutual funds. Be sure to scrutinize the charges before deciding to invest in one.

Mutual funds have raked in many adversities due to the expensive fees associated with actively managed funds. The ones that are actively managed don't have paying for the staff that continually studies as well as trades with the funds, and as a result, they pay less costs and costs.

Similar to that ETFs that are managed by passive means also have lower fees. They're great for retirement funds because high fees could slowly reduce the gains, particularly in the case of a long-term retirement plan. However, there's a need to be cautious as not all ETFs are managed passively and there are active managed ETFs also and they are something to avoid buying.

Certain ETFs track their index in full that invests in every the stocks that are available. For instance, that of the SPDR S&P 500 ETF. Some investors only invest in a few of the stocks that belong to their specific indices such as that of the Vanguard Total Stock Market ETF.

Do some further study before placing your money into an ETF because both strategies can produce different outcomes. You could, for instance, examine the ways in which an ETF index operates and see how it's performance compared against the index it is based on. Be aware of the fees they charge as well.

Mutual funds are different from. ETFs

If both your mutual fund as well as ETF are monitoring the performance of an index, the results may not be impressive. The main consideration is to whether you'd prefer to invest a lesser amount over a period of period of time or invest a large amount all at all at.

If you're looking to invest an enormous amount in one go for instance, let's say that you're participating in the 401(k) as well as an IRA rollover, then an ETF is the best route to take. In contrast it is possible to invest $200 every month (or any other small amount that you invest sporadically over time) an ordinary mutual fund is the more suitable option.

To get rid of the hassle of commissions and fees, you may want to consider making contact with an discount broker. The person you choose to contact is a traditional stock broker who purchases and sells orders for lower commission rates.

Prior to the advent of the internet, access to brokers was only available to those with a lot of money. However, with the advancement of technology in communications and the internet, there is an explosion in brokers available to everyone, including people with less funds to trade at reduced commission rates.

One important thing to remember is that discount brokers do not provide any kind of research, advice or even a personal service to customers. They simply take orders. This is the reason they be able to offer a lower commission as opposed to full-service brokers. You can always conduct your own research, or seek advice from a discount broker which has no cost.

Another financial investment option that I suggest to diversify your portfolio and decrease the risk level of this portfolio are Treasury Bonds (or T-bonds). They're not just reliable and safe investments , you also get a constant rate of interest throughout the entire term of the bond unlike equity. Additionally, you do not have to pay tax to the state government or the federal government on the interest you earn.

Because they are backed through the credit line of the Federal government, they're very secure. The yields are expected to earn for the majority of Treasury bonds are tied with the 5-year Treasury rate. The time frames can be very long and they also have a low annual rate of return. However, even in this case they beat inflation that has been hovering around 2 percent for quite a while.

T-bonds shouldn't comprise more than the smallest percentage of your portfolio in the case of being young. The precise percentage will be determined by the risk profile of your. If you're in or near your retirement, the proportion of your portfolio for T-bonds must be higher. This is because it's an assured stream of income and, when combined together with the other choices, can give you enough money to avoid the burden of debt after retirement and help you pay your bills.

Learnings from Investment Lessons with COVID

The COVID-19 epidemic has led to disasters that are unjustified in their magnitude. There's been numerous losses It's not surprising that people who are about to retire are afraid of what's to come and how they can stop the loss of their retirement savings to waste.

To give you an idea studies and surveys (Morningstar 2020) have proven that everything from equity to US stock to foreign Stocks were unable to make money in the first quarter of. Bonds aren't a secure choice, in any way because they have a low yield. In the past, traditional retirement accounts have lost approximately one-third of the funds and anything greater than 10% of a loss for people nearing retirement is considered to be excessive.

The only places where your cash can be considered secure are US bonds, treasuries and gold, because they've been able to defend themselves well from the COVID-19 lockdown consequences. Therefore, the best thing to do is now not to be taking risks however, to reduce it as likely as you can, and take care to limit damage.

The traditional target-date funds have helped people somewhat However, this isn't the time to be sitting around and let the market dictate how your retirement will play out. You need to be actively involved in the way your portfolio is designed and managed. Consider advice on your finances from the top experts you can locate.

Make your portfolio unique based on your preferences and the market's conditions. As often as you can, and keep commissions and fees to the minimal. If you're near your Risk Zone, it is ideal to decrease the percentage of equity within your portfolio.

In the end, what we're seeing with regard to COVID-19 is the weaknesses of our traditional retirement plan. The 60/40 rule is outdated and you ought at the more intelligent investment opportunities the world offers.

Important lessons to take away

There isn't a universal plan that works for everyone any more. Based on your personal capacity you need to split your portfolio into bonds, ETFs, mutual funds, and stocks and diversify as far that you are able to. Don't put all your eggs in one basket , and ensure that no one investment makes up more than 4 percent of your portfolio. So, you'll be safe from market's downturns and remain strong even during serious crises, such as pandemics.

A good example of a well-diversified Portfolio

Investment Type Percentage of Portfolio

US Large-Cap Stocks 25%

US Small-Cap Stocks 20%

Foreign Developed Stocks 15%

Diversified Real Estate 15%

Diversified Bonds 10%

Foreign Emerging Stocks 10%

Diversified Commodities 5%

Chapter 9: 6 Tried & Tested Steps To Find

how to choose the Right Financial Advisor

T

A good financial advisor can transform your financial situation and assist you with much more than just advising and researching on investment options. The hiring process should be a planned process, to allow you to collaborate with them for many years. It might take some time, and that is normal but the time you put into it will be worthwhile and bring you security knowing that your retirement savings and funds will be well-taken to ensure your retirement.

This chapter I'll explain six steps I've tried and tested through the years to help you choose the best financial consultant.

Step 1: Determine the issues you require help in

You should know the issues you require help in, as we've gone through many of the information you could want to research through and learn about particular investment options in depth prior to making any investment.

There are three main types of financial advisors that offer the guidance you're seeking. They provide the following services: they provide:

* Financial planning is a aspect of your financial life which determines how much you can save and what kind of insurance you need. It's not just about the investment you invest in, but also how you can save your money.

* Investment advisory services focus on investment management decisions like which investments to purchase and which accounts could be used to do this. The ongoing process of financial planning will allow you to select the most suitable investment option.

* The retirement income plan focuses on how you can connect and coordinate the various elements of your financial life like retirement, taxes, investments, Social Security, the date you will retire and other such things to ensure that they are all integrated well and contribute to the same goal, which is to provide periodic paychecks for the duration of your retirement.

If you're not in the market for extensive financial advice, you can consider an automated advisor since it's inexpensive and doesn't need an enormous opening balance. A robo-advisor is an online platform that provides recommendations based on algorithms for financial planning and streamlines the entire process, meaning there's no need for human oversight or intervention. A basic robo-advisor would ask you to provide information regarding your financial situation as well as your goals via a questionnaire and then make use of the information you supply to create guidance and to invest your assets automatically.

Step 2: Look for Financial Advisors that have

Reputable Credentials

You may have noticed that financial advisors are able to use various letters that go with their names. They are certified and designations that show their skills. There are over 100 different certifications and designations that financial advisors can boast to stand out and get recruited. However, not all of these certifications mean the exact things.

There are some companies which offer qualifications that are easy to acquire for a commission and permit salespeople to look as experts. This is why I'm going to inform you about three trustworthy qualifications, which should, if a financial adviser is at least one, will offer you the confidence that you're working with a reliable financial advisor.

Certified Financial Planner (CFP)

If a financial adviser is certified with the CFP certification You can be confident that you are hiring the right person to do the job. This is because CFP experts are CFP professional is bound to strict conditions and standards set in place by the Certified Financial Planner Board of Standards, Inc. The CFP candidate must have an education, pass rigorous tests, have expertise, and the ethical standards to be awarded the credential.

The conduct standards, in accordance with the Fitness Standards for Registrants and Candidates make sure that financial advisors who are qualified put the needs of their clients in mind.

Chartered Financial Analyst (CFA)

A lot of financial advisors hold the prestigious designation CFA that is awarded from the CFA institute, which is internationally recognized. If you need help with your investment research and managing the portfolio of your investments, only other option better than an CFA qualified financial professional. To earn this certification an applicant must fulfill the academic, exam and practical requirements like the CFP.

The CFA must also adhere to ethical guidelines set in CFA Institute. CFA Institute. That means that you can be guaranteed to receive top-quality financial advice from an CFA approved financial advisor.

Personal Financial Specialist (PFS)

This certification is only available to those who have completed their studies in retirement planning as well as insurance and estate planning, investments and other areas of personal financial planning.

PFS is an accredited credential that is considered as highly and highly by members of the American Institute of Certified Public Accountants. Financial advisors must undergo a rigorous and professional training as well as three years or more of professional experience as well as strict ethical standards. As with the other certificates we discussed earlier, PFS advisors too have be able to pass an examination in order to be eligible for the position.

Step 3: Know How Financial

Advisors Are Compensated

The credentials financial advisors possess matter greatly in determining whether you've got the most qualified person to do the job. Beyond the credentials, you must consider the method that the financial advisor will be paid.

There are a variety of ways that financial planners are compensated however you should go for the one that is 'Fee Only' because this is the most effective choice, particularly when you look at what alternatives are. Pay attention to this as there's a huge distinction between "Fee Based" and "Fee Only the compensations.

We've previously discussed commission-based financial planners who earn profits from their financial services they offer. They're employed by big financial institutions , and their pre-planned bundles that they sell to retired people, are what helps them earn money.

However Fee-based advisors are different kind of advisor. They are a new breed of advisors that are associated with brokers and agents similar to commission-based counterparts, they also have licenses to offer financial products on commission. Their advice can be difficult for someone looking for a personalised advice in light of the financial circumstances of their clients, since they also earn a commission by the quantity of products they sell.

On the other side There are Fee Only advisors, which is the only kind of financial advisor is recommended to clients for complete financial planning and/or asset management. It is the responsibility of these financial advisors be in the best interests of their clients.

They're compensated for their services on an hourly basis , or by an amount of the assets they manage. The advisors do not receive compensation or commission for the financial products they offer, which is why they generally provide more extensive guidance.

If you choose to work with a Fee Only financial advisor they are paid in a fixed-rate arrangement and they can plan annual reviews. This allows you to receive advice all year.

Step 4: Find an Advisor

Finding the best financial advisor isn't difficult to solve. However, you must be aware of the things you need to know in relation to your objectives. I suggest speaking to family members and friends about the goals you want to achieve by consulting with a financial adviser.

There could be things you didn't realize that your family and acquaintances could be capable of revealing. This will greatly help define your goals and put your financial situation into an objective perspective. With the right questions you can ask a financial professional and you'll be able to begin searching for one.

Your friends might be able to provide you with advice on which financial adviser you should consult. Be aware that taking the advice doesn't mean you're bound to the advisors. If they don't seem right or their ethics or recommendations don't match what you want to achieve Don't hesitate to explore an advisor who's style you prefer.

One good site to search for a financial adviser is NAPFA.org. You can search for a variety of financial advisors within your area through this site. NAPFA is the largest professional organization of advisors who are paid on a 'fee only basis.

This is the ideal spot to go to if you've not had financial advice before and want someone to help without the hassle of having to deal by the responsibilities. A fee-only approach to compensation will let you stay clear from any contracts or salesmanship that are thrown at you, and get expert advice in accordance with your particular needs.

Do not limit yourself to just a few names when looking for financial experts. Make a list of people who are located within your vicinity and perform an old-fashioned search on each name in the list. Visit their website to discover all the details you can on their profiles, including bios as well as the services they provide. Don't forget to read through the small text.

Another method to get information on the financial advisors you have on your list is to go to the U.S. Securities and Exchange Commission (SEC) website at sec.gov. On the home page located in the upper right corner, enter your name and the number of the financial adviser whom you wish to contact.

After this, you'll receive a full review of the advisor's activities as well as their previous employers as well as any disciplinary actions taken by the SEC has initiated against the advisor. You can then sift through the information quickly to find an advisor who is professional and has a good track of record.

The next thing that I highly recommend you to do, is to visit the Financial Industry Regulatory

Authority (FINRA) website at brokercheck.finra.org. Enter your name and the title of the financial adviser you are considering and learn about the number of years of experience they've had.

On the site on the website, you can also information about their education and the number of professional exams they have cleared, and whether they hold an official license from the state (which is crucial).

Finally, ensure that the financial advisor is fiduciary. If an advisor's status is fiduciary this means that they are supported with the SEC or other appropriate government authorities to only work in your best interest. There are instances where advisors are stockbrokers as well as financial advisors.

The problem is that stockbrokers do not legally required to adhere to the exact SEC fiduciary obligations that financial advisors must meet. This is why it's essential to choose a broker that is a fiduciary and is supported by the appropriate authorities.

Step 5: Do a Background Check

Although I've provided couple of resources to help you conduct background checks on the financial advisors you have selected I'd want to reiterate this point and offer the resources once more.

The financial advisor needs to be backed through FINRA or by the SEC. If it is FINRA, then you can use the https://brokercher.finra.org/. If a financial adviser works as a broker, or is an agent of a broker they are controlled by FINRA.

If it is the SEC, you can use https://www.sec.gov/. If a financial advisor is employed as an investment advisor, the advisor will be subject to regulation under the SEC or by the local securities authorities.

On these websites You can discover whether the financial advisor is associated with any broker. You can also discover if there have been any criminal actions or disciplinary action taken against the advisor.

FINRA even has a page (finra.org/investors/professional-designations) dedicated that lists each reputed designation that a financial advisor can have as well as the organization that issues those designations.

Check that the person you're hiring has legitimate credentials because there have been a number of instances where 'experts' and advisors' relied on credentials they didn't have to scam money out of retired people.

Another way that you can conduct an investigation into the background of the financial advisors you have enlisted is to conduct a search on the internet. Use the search engine you prefer and enter the advisor's names (or their company's names) and then add terms like "complaint" and "lawsuit.'

Check the results of your search and check for any allegations or instances against the individuals. You can also use the latest social media platforms like LinkedIn which allows users to network with each other and discover whether your financial advisor is using the site.

The majority of the time you'll see trustworthy financial advisors who communicate with their clients online and also give back to the community too. Their profile pages should provide enough information to determine whether they're reliable.

Step 6: Interview Them

If you do decide to select a financial advisor make sure you interview them thoroughly and ask questions regarding their qualifications and experience and discover whether they're worthy of your trust. Here are 10 questions you can ask them, and the reasons why you should ask them.

1. Are you a fiduciary?

This is the most important question to ask over other questions since you should not be able to trust any financial professional who isn't fiduciary. Fiduciary status means that an advisor's job is to be regulated by authorities of the state to act only in your best interests.

2. Will you always be fiduciary?

This may seem to be a little snarky to certain people, but it's nonetheless an important question. Fiduciaries are legally required to be a fiduciary by SEC to act to serve your best interests and financial advisors are required to keep doing this for the period for which you are paying them. If you believe that your advisor is trying to adhere to their own agenda You have the right to terminate their relationship with you.

3. Are you able to provide the signature of a document confirming your agreement to act as fiduciary?

In the end, you're trying to build a rapport with the financial advisor in order that you can share with the advisor what your personal financial goals are and how they can assist you in the most effective way.

To achieve this there's no shame in asking them to submit a written document to declare their agreement to be an fiduciary. It is likely that they should not be concerned should be their intention and you're paying them for it.

4. How many years have you been a financial advisor for?

The rationale behind this question is simple It's because you're looking to gain the assistance of an expert financial advisor. Your financial advisor should not be able to answer the question.

The organizations that validate their credentials require at least three years of experience. any more than that must be considered a good thing. Even if the candidate isn't more experienced than others should not be put off from hiring them so long as you feel they are skilled and easy to work with.

5. Do you have a lot of clients affected by the 2007 or 2008 financial meltdowns?

The reason you need to ask this question is to see whether your financial advisor experienced difficult times. These were among the most challenging times for financial advisors to work in (today's financial situation is similar to those). If the advisor had clients during the past who emerged fairly unscathed and sane, then you can be sure that you're talking to an expert.

6. If you would like to speak to those clients who were there through those tough times.

This inquiry because many financial advisors are quick to blow their own horn to appear professional. To distinguish the grains from the chaff it is best to ask this inquiry and then check if the advisor is willing to take the initiative. This should reveal much about the professionality of the advisor and character, but also the character of the advisor.

7. How many customers do you have coming up on retirement?

Answering this query ought to reveal how suitable your financial advisor will be to you. The more clients in the near-retirement phase your financial advisor is able to handle more clients, the better it will be for you since this will mean that the advisor is experienced in this specific field and can assist you in achieving your goals more effectively.

8. Is my portfolio size typical?

This query should prompt your financial advisor to look through your investment portfolio, and suggesting things based on what your approach to investing is. Even if the size of your portfolio isn't typical and your financial advisor will offer suggestions with regard to the size of your portfolio.

9. How do I pay you? What exactly is that cost?

This is an extremely important question you should ask the financial adviser you trust. In essence, you're asking if the financial advisor is payed per hour per visit, or in a different way. It should be discussed between you (you may also include your loved ones and friends as well) at the start.

Apart from that you must also try for the possibility that there are additional hidden charges and, if yes and what they are. It is essential that everything is as transparent as they can be so that you are able to move on and establish a relationship to your advisor in the financial world on which trust and advice will be based.

10. Which is the custodian?

In the ideal scenario your financial advisor could have employed an independent custodian to manage funds instead of acting as their own custodian. This is an important test that will ensure that the financial advisor is accountable.

If an advisor is able to provide you with your information about your investment performance and informs you of the amount you have in your account it is easy to visit the internet within a minute and verify if the information is accurate or not.

The prospect of meeting with your financial advisor could cause you to be nervous. However, it's important to be aware that the advisor's already anticipating it. In the end, it's the beginning of a relationship developing with someone. Questions should be asked to determine if the advisor is the right one for you.

Inform the advisor that you're taking a look at them, so they are aware that you won't make a quick decision. This shouldn't cause you to be nervous since it's you who will select them.

If you're not confident in having confidence in handling the details of your financial situation but you should still be capable of asking questions and ask candidates for the job. In the end, it's you are paying your financial advisor to understand your financial picture and not make it even more confusing. If you think your advisor is causing confusion it is your right to quit at any point.

Important key

In the end the hiring process for an advisor for financial services should be considered with some thought and investigation. Of course, it is important to know precisely what you require help with. What's even more crucial is contacting someone with the appropriate qualifications, experience ethics, and experience to provide you the advice you require.

I suggest you choose financial advisors that are compensated by the basis of a fee Only basis. This will guarantee that you are not being pressured into buying financial products or to accept a price that is excessive. Conducting a thorough background search together in asking questions the selected applicants, will help you to select who is the best candidate to fill the position.

The reason Fiduciary Advisors are highly recommended

Suitability Advisor Fiduciary Advisor

Advice Provide 'suitable advice' that is in the best interests of the client

Regulatory Oversight Suitability Rule - FINRA Compliance SEC or Individual States

Revenues Received Commissions, as well as fees not disclosed by Insurance or Investment Companies Fees for the Services Provided be disclosed and transparent

Conflicts of Interest You do not need to be described or reveal. You must identify and disclose

Costs Not required to take into consideration costs to clients. However, it is important to consider the cost to clients

Serving your Best Interests Standard for Lower Clients. Highest Standard of Clients Best Interest

Chapter 10: Your Legacy To The World

In the final section, I'd like to discuss the subject of leaving the legacy of a loved one, which can be very emotional for many. Nobody wants to think about the day they'll need to pass on their possessions to their children and say goodbye however it is essential to do so.

Have you ever considered what is the meaning behind leaving an inheritance? Most likely, it involves leaving the possessions we have to our beloved family members. However, there's much beyond the fact that. It's how you'll be remembered by the people who are following you, in general. There are some aspects which can be categorized as real or not.

Your possessions and money leaving to your loved ones, which requires estate planning. Everything else - all of your memories, the work you contribute to the community and the care, love and wisdom that you offer - makes your legacy outlast any possessions you might leave behind.

However, that doesn't mean you should not be concerned about the practical aspect of it, because this is definitely something that requires some kind of planning from you So I'll begin by focusing on that aspect first.

Having an Estate Plan

The process of preparing an estate plan involves getting all your legal papers in order that outline the way the wealth you've amassed will left to your loved ones following your death. It also specifies what you'd like others to do to take care of your financial and health care decisions in the event you're not capable of doing so in the final stage that you live.

A comprehensive estate plan can help you feel confident about the future. It is a guarantee that your loved family members will be taken care of and that the legacy your family leaves is line to your wishes.

An extensive estate plan will ensure you reduce probate and taxes fees to ensure that your loved ones don't have to worry about anything after you're gone. In the absence of a plan, it will cause a lot of problems and confusion for your family members. So let's glance at some primary advantages from having an estate strategy.

Protecting Beneficiaries

A few years ago planning an estate was something only high net worth people needed. However, the things have evolved. The majority of middle-class families need an estate plan for the eventuality of the death of the family member who is the main breadwinner. You don't need to be super-rich to succeed in the realm of real estate or the stock market. And since you may have assets that you can pass to the next generation and on, an estate plan is an essential thing to have.

Even if all you leave behind is your second residence and you're not in control of who gets the property when you pass away and you don't get to have any control over the fate of the property. In essence, you're letting forces of time and tide determine how the house is treated you have put your money into.

If you do not have an estate planning plan The courts will be able to determine who gets your property. The process could take many years, accrue numerous fees and get very unpleasant. The courts will not be able to determine which child is the most responsible, and which child should not have the same access to these resources. The courts can't decide automatically that the spouse who survives receives everything, either.

Protecting Young Children

No one thinks about young people getting old and dying. However, if you've got children who are young, you need to prepare for the unimaginable. Here is you will need to consider the Will portion of your estate plan comes into play.

A formal estate plan will assure that your kids are looked after by the way you would like and are comfortable with. The estate plan must include named the guardians for your children in the event that both parents die before children turn the age of. If you do not name the guardians, the issue will be decided by the court and the court will determine who gets to take care of your children.

Saving your heirs from a huge tax bill

You're looking to safeguard your loved ones when you're gone. That's the place your estate plan can help. The majority of it involves safeguarding your loved ones from IRS. A crucial element in your will is the transfer of your assets to descendants while making sure it is a minimal tax burden on them.

Even the worst estate plans could allow your heirs to cut some of their state inheritance tax and tax on estates that are federal or state. Without an estate arrangement, the total amount your heirs may be liable to the government could be quite substantial.

Eliminating Family Messes

The tales have already been reported: A person who has money dies. This creates conflict between the family members. One sibling may think that he has more right than others, or another might think they should have the responsibility of finances, even though they're in the process of accumulating debt. Discords that arise from unresolved estate issues can become unpalatable and ugly, and eventually end up in the courtroom.

Stopping these disputes before they begin is another reason you must plan out the manner in which your estate will be divided. This will let you manage your financial assets and assets in the event that the worst happens and you fall ill or in the event of your passing away. It can also go in the direction of putting any rifts between your family members and assures that your assets are taken care of in the way you want to be handled.

In addition, it creates individual plans for your loved family members. You can arrange for those who have health issues or establish trusts for those who do not have the most prudent financial habits and are not able to be trusted with large sums of money. In addition, it lets you pay back more towards the kid who looked out for you during your final days.

It is not necessary to distribute the distribution of your estate among your heirs. However, doing this is among the most important issues you need to consider. If the totality of your estate and the beneficiaries are numerous (or the beneficiaries include more than one spouse or family members) this is the most pressing issue you must be thinking about.

You should at least know what amount of funds you have and what your expected life expectation should be based on your medical and medical history. With that knowledge we can examine the essential 6 documents you need to plan your estate.

#1: Will

It's perhaps the most common document you can have in your estate plan. It will identify your personal representative, or an executor who will oversee and distribute your estate assets in the you want. The will may also specify whom will act as the guardians for your children who are minors (if they exist) and who will care for them until they become adults.

#2: Revocable or Living Trust

Trusts can help with the ability to manage your assets while you're alive, as well as the names of the people who will be the beneficiaries of your assets after your death. Trusts like these can help in planning in the event that you are to become disabled. In certain states, they can even help simplify probate. Although living trusts do offer advantages but there are some issues (such funeral wishes) that are only addressed through the will.

#3: Personal Property Memorandum

Based on the location you reside in depending on where you live, this document can allow you to leave some of your chattels including jewelry, artwork furniture, things to those not listed by your will. This document isn't so formal or official as your will and may be modified at any point.

#4: Durable Power of Attorney

This document permits you to designate a family member, friend member or an advisor who will be identified as an agent who will handle legal and financial issues in your name.

#5: Health Care Proxy, Power of Attorney, or Agent

This document lets you nominate a trusted person take health decisions for you if you're no longer capable of doing so. This document automatically grants the person access to your medical record. Take note that some institutions may require that they be able to provide more proof to gain access to all medical documents.

#6: Living Will

The type of will you choose to use is designed to cover your final wishes . It is different in comparison to your medical proxy. Living wills generally cover pain relief as well as the possibility of utilizing ventilators, resuscitations or feeding tubes.

Although having the appropriate legal documents is essential to plan your estate however, it's not all. Based on the complexity of your property is might need to consult with your attorney and financial advisor when making the estate plans.

It is also crucial to review and revise regularly your estate plan. Law changes, particularly on the federal level, regarding estate taxes, as well as other changes in your life like the death or birth of a family member divorce, or marriage could require you to review the plan you have in place.

It is important to know the importance of estate planning and it's not a sole right of the wealthy. If you do not own an extravagant house or costly things to pass the family members you love in the absence of an estate strategy,, it could be extremely difficult the loved ones of your family to sort out your estate after you die.

Your legacy does not begin and end with the things your family leaves behind. Whatever important your possessions be, the real significance of your legacy stems from things that don't possess a formal form, items that are left in the minds of others and what they imagine as they consider your life. Your home or your material possessions and everything else can be viewed and weighed. However, true legacy is important, because it's by your charitable acts your interactions, your kindness, or your generous spirit that you'll be remembered by the people who will be left behind.

Don't Forget to be Generous

The stingy and financially strained years should not stop you from giving your heart's desire for the rest of your life. You've reached the point that you are able to give as much as you want. You've got x amount of money in your account, and you've earned a profit from your investments, and all essential financial elements are in place to provide for your needs. However, your life isn't over simply because you've retired. In fact, it's just begun.

The present moment of your life isn't like anything else you've had before. Your concerns and desires are completely different from the way they used to be. You can now dedicate more time to the things you've always wanted to accomplish. In addition, you'll have the tools available to help others.

This is the perfect moment to be involved with philanthropy and charitable causes or simply show your appreciation to those and things that are pulling at your heart. Although you may have plenty of time to yourself, sharing it with others is going bring the most enjoyment out out of you too. Be involved in the community and help them by volunteering your time and money.

People who are in the final stages of adulthood and in the midst of old age are the ones who have the greatest impact on society because they're the guardians of the past, experts and, naturally financially secure people that help them transfer their wisdom and knowledge to the next generation.

I'd suggest you give as freely in your giving as your heart will allow since it will not only create an unbroken chain of generations of knowledge, but it also provides you with a sense of satisfaction and respect which is reserved by society for those who've had for a long time.

Key Takeaways

Making an estate plan is an undertaking which requires a lot of contemplation and consideration in order to leave the legacy of happiness and happiness, not one of petty conflict and division.

Making sure you have all the essential estate plan documents and contingency plans will not only save you from a pile of headaches to tackle in the future It will provide your loved ones with the peace of mind being assured that everything is made in accordance with your wishes.

If your estate is substantial and you have a lot of grandchildren, children, and individuals to whom you would like to leave your property, I recommend you speak with attorneys and financial advisors to assist you in drafting your will. Their experience in these areas can help you be able to get right down to the details, make it easier to manage the issues, and plan for unexpected events.

While the whole procedure can be very difficult for the soul, particularly in the event of selling the home and moving to a new one, it's an action that must be done in the direction of forward movement rather than in the back. Be generous by giving your time and your resources. Your loved ones, your community family members, as well as the entire world is in need of you.

Chapter 11: To Retire, Or Not To Retire

Everybody ages and those who are hard-working and make sacrifices every day, eventually will develop wrinkles and gray hair. This isn't about the physical consequences of aging, however. It's about the evolution of your worth and the certainty that one day you'll enjoy the fruits of your hard work. It's impossible to control ageing since it's among the most natural phenomena on earth, but the one thing you control but that is the way you be living your life after you're old enough to retire.

Retirement is a subject that young people think about since it's the time when people can have the total freedom to choose the direction he wants to take and what to do with the remainder of their lives with the hard-earned cash he's saved. Retirement is an amazing time to re-discover yourself, and If you're unsure if you'll retire at all or not It's a good idea to look into the suggestions below.

Why Retire?

Imagine driving one car for the remainder all your lives. The car might be an efficient and reliable vehicle during the initial few years, but with time, its performance is beginning to diminish. It's not because the vehicle isn't in good condition or that you've been a negligent and unreliable owner. the car just needs to be retired.

It is possible to compare a person's retirement partially to the automobile or other gadget. There comes a point at which you need to reduce or even stop working as you have for the last two or three decades, and have a restful break. It's good to know that you won't be taken to the junkyard to be shredded and reused. There is a possibility to take a vacation, a long one.

Retirement doesn't symbolize inefficiency and age. It is actually the reward to people who have put in the effort to survive and support families. If you're a man, or woman, you should be able to retire, and be able to begin your life that you are productive.

Retirement is the time to enjoy peace to your life. You've spent way too many hours at the office, and making sure that your bosses and subordinates are pleased with the work you do. You've spent a lot of time worried about your company's longevity and the efficiency of the business's director. You've made a significant contribution and made the possible for a lot of people to live a better life. Isn't it about time to begin making yourself a priority?

Although retirement doesn't mean a major shift of focus from the rest of society to yours it's a privilege that isn't available to all. A lot of people don't attain retirement because they die. Many prefer to stay in their jobs due to the competitive business world. Some are unable to retire, as they have many expenses to pay for.

They're just excuses, but. If one is determined to retire, there is a way. A lot of people are successful in retirement regardless of the situation they had to face prior to achieving this final goal. If you've got a strong goal of retiring now, you're a step closer to reaching it. When you've started to ask your self questions about the "why's" of retirement, you'll discover that "because."

Unnecessary Retirement Theories

What is the reason that so many people aren't interested in retirement? It's because their opinions and values aren't insubstantial. But, the same convictions can be used to assist you in moving forward to retirement and live a better life. There isn't any set method to ensure a prosperous retirement or preparing for it knowing what you shouldn't be a part of can help guide you in the right direction.

A few people do not want to retire due to the fear of being unable to identify themselves. Identity is often tied to the profession or work and this can lead to the disadvantaging of retirement-related concerns. Many people aren't even thinking about retiring , even though they would be living a fulfilling life beyond the confines of their messy offices and bustling conference rooms. Retirement isn't a cause to lose your identity, but. In many instances, it assists you in finding the last piece of the puzzle that aid in completing your identity. Allowing yourself to quit the workplace and give up your job and let your life flow in the way you want to lead you to new possibilities; that you did not even think existed.

A second major concern for those who don't want to retire is about the stability of their finances. Many believe that if they quit their jobs and take a break, the bills will not be paid but the mortgage will not go away and the college funds won't be sufficient. Financial stability does not solely depend on job security, but. If you invest wisely and save money--this is covered in the next chapter--you don't have to think about your bills or other financial issues.

Many are reluctant to retire due to the fear that they'll stop learning and growing. Actually, the opposite is true. Retirement offers a variety of avenues to grow meaningfully. Because you have all the time in the world, your learning is entirely dependent on your ability to be flexible. You're now conscious that your life as well as time will be your principal instructors. They've always taught you, in fact. But people are often too busy with their lives that they overlook the core of joy and fulfillment.

You're getting older, but you're still far from being completely aware of everything that is happening in the world. You'll never be short of things to explore and take note of. Retirement opens your eyes, mind as well as your heart, to new type of beauty. The beauty of this was hidden from view by the hectic shifts meetings, meetings, paper work and deadlines. However, you are now in the an open seat to see all that is.

Essentials to Remember When Considering Retirement

After you've realized that retirement is an alternative that's equally viable it's important to look at some of the essentials. As you've probably been told, retirement planning doesn't begin until a few years prior to your actual retirement date. Be aware that the earlier you begin planning for retirement, the better it will be in store for you once you're done with those suits and office and into the wonderful retirement life.

It's a good idea to establish what "retired" you looks like. What are you planning to do once you are retired? There's no specific method to retire, and you don't need to follow what your coworkers or other relatives who have retired have accomplished. Determine your retirement timeframe to better plan for it. It is a matter of knowing your self a bit more. The process of self-discovery will lead to a greater knowledge of what makes your whole.

Perhaps the first thing that comes to the mind is a long vacation in the tropical paradise, golfing or more hours watching television. Whatever your ideal retirement plan you must prepare. It's the key to allow you to open the doors you've always wanted to walk through. Don't think you'll have a wonderful retirement if your planning isn't appropriately. To give yourself a present and your loved ones do not forget to consider the aspects of your life that could influence your retirement. Make sure you invest in your retirement as you'll be the main beneficiary of these preparations.

There are some who can't include their family's opinions into the equation when considering retirement. They think about what will make them feel happy and how they'll feel when they stop waking up earlier in the day and working. It is advisable not to think about yourself as your loved ones might be eager to join in and help you.

Your relationships must be taken into consideration when planning your retirement. Your spouse might not be used to seeing you at home all of the time , or your children may have a different view of what you consider to be your "retirement persona" than what you really envision. Be sure to carefully and quickly let your family and friends know the reason you'll retire in the near future or in the near future. So, some adjustments could be made, and you could even see what retirement offers after you're done.

Prior to making planning, we should be aware that a fulfilling and fulfilling life cannot be experienced during retirement. When you're preparing for your retirement, be aware that every day presents an opportunity to make a difference in people's lives, especially your own. Every day at work can be a chance to leave a an impact on the world. Every minute counts, in fact. Don't stop at preparing for retirement, but also continue to grow and discover ways to enjoy your life as you go along.

Chapter 12: Retirement Preparations

When you have decided to retire is the best way to go, a thorough planning becomes essential. Michael Baisden's quote, "Those who fail to plan, plan to fail," is a logical assertion that can keep in mind two essential necessity: preparation and planning. When you think about and plan for the majority of events in your life and the lives of those you love and your loved ones, you should take the same approach with regard to your retirement.

The process might not be as simple as it's laid out in numerous retirement books, but focusing on important aspects will make it easier to understand the steps. It's all about being financially prepared to make the right choices even after retirement and the smart decision-making process for managing money. It's no more Advanced Physics and Chemistry, however, prudence and shrewd judgement are needed.

Are You Financially Ready?

Many people are enticed to become the financial advisors of their choice, and rely on calculators online for stock and assets. They believe that simply because they have hard-earned money as well as savings that they will automatically have a handle on how to use it. Many have failed in this fight. Many people ended up living beyond their savings because they did not consult a financial planner who was a professional to provide reliable, quality guidance.

It is generally not a good idea to be confident when it comes to managing their wealth. Furthermore, because this is their personal money, they will not be able to determine whether they're financially secure or not. If you have an amount of $20,000 on your bank account to save, will you be able to determine the most effective option to make use of or invest it? If you're certain--and If you're a professional financial planner, then you can you can go ahead. But, if you're not, consult an professional.

Most, mainly males, are reluctant to let someone else take the decision or offer viable paths in the management of their own finances. There are a lot of fake financial advisers on the market and there are many who truly want to assist you. Research trustworthy financial planners or companies who can guide you through the complicated and confusing world that can be referred to as"the "market."

A more practical and useful financial plan can be found when you rely on an expert. He can assist you in distributing your money in a way that you be able to gain a lot over the long term and avoid many financial traps. When you were able to have a teacher while you were young and have a mentor in the present who's helping you prepare for retirement is also crucial. It is possible to help one another out and establish a reliable and secure path towards an enjoyable retirement.

Many are scared to allow someone else to review their financial statements However, being honest is essential in this scenario. If you've not been a prudent manage of your wealth in the past, but salvation is not far away. If you've been unable to invest wisely and effectively manage your money means you need help from a professional.

Make sure that you have financial stability as an essential element to have a peacefuland happy retirement. You'll be unable to fully enjoy every minute of your existence if you're deeply in debt and your bills keep increasing. Do not be worried about the potential negatives, since a happy retirement is also feasible. It's more likely to have a stable financial situation when you retire if you have an accurate picture of your financial situation. You'll be able to determine the steps you should do once you're aware of the right steps to take and avoid.

Annuities in Your Portfolio

Annuities are contracts that exist between insurance firms and individuals planning to retire. They are intended to assist you in achieve long-term financial goals that also form the basis for a successful retirement. If you're looking to ensure the availability of a constant stream of cash when you retire, think about including annuities in your portfolio.

The risk tolerance you have in the stock market diminishes with time, so it's advisable to build up your savings. Financial planners and investors tend towards investing in "Deferred Annuity." This is basically a kind of Annuity in which payments of installments or massive sums of money are held back until the investor decides whether or not to be able to receive the funds.

The type of annuity you choose has two phases which are the savings and income phase. The first step involves placing money in your account. The second phase involves the transformation of the plan to an annuity. In the next phase you will begin receiving cash payments from your investment. The most important thing you need to be aware of is that an Annuity can provide an income tax deduction. The tax deduction will be deferred until you decide to cash out the funds. Because the tax deduction is significantly less this means you'll save money and also have more to invest in your retirement.

Nowadays, a savings account won't suffice because prices of various commodities-- necessities and other products and services-- continue to increase. There are many who have a lack of self-control when it comes to saving and spending their money. Few people can truly claim to be wise with their spending and a consistent saver, but anyone who receives each month a paycheck can choose to include annuities in their portfolio.

This opportunity isn't only available to a few. Whatever number of numbers your monthly income is you can put it into your retirement by purchasing annuities. Given the inherent fluctuation of the stock market, this strategy is regarded as essential by a lot of individuals who are looking for a secure retirement. Additionally, because this system was specifically designed for people who are planning to retire it's a sensible investment in the financial future. The money you earn can be used for your benefit even if you're not spending it on your current requirements. In reality, the portion of your net worth that will be the most significant factor in your retirement is the part which isn't in your pocket or in your hands right now.

A Working Retirement

A few people believe that they can continue to work until they retire. The job however, is totally different from the previous one. Experience and wisdom do come with age, and they aren't letting their slower and muscular body keep them from their goals. The brain gets stronger when you get older, as the physical and psychological strength are in inverse proportion.

* 9 7 8 1 9 9 8 9 0 1 6 5 4 *